Partners in Wisdom and Grace

Catechesis and Religious Education in Dialogue

Marylin T. Kravatz

University Press of America,® Inc.
Lanham • Boulder • New York • Toronto • Plymouth, UK

University Press of America,® Inc.
4501 Forbes Boulevard
Suite 200
Lanham, Maryland 20706
UPA Acquisitions Department (301) 459-3366

Estover Road
Plymouth PL6 7PY
United Kingdom

Library of Congress Control Number: 2009935797
ISBN: 978-0-7618-4938-4 (paperback : alk. paper)
eISBN: 978-0-7618-4939-1

To my parents, Helen DeBrosky and David Swartz, whose love and interreligious marriage provided me with a true religious education.

Contents

Acknowledgments

Authoring a book of this type is accomplished with the collaboration, support, encouragement, wisdom, and academic expertise of people who leave lifelong impressions. I am most grateful to have had such people who were willing to join me on this journey.

I am privileged to have been a student of some of finest teachers in the fields of catechesis and religious education. I am especially grateful to the faculty of Fordham University's Graduate School of Religion and Religious Education who brought me to new horizons of learning. I will always be indebted to Kieran Scott, Ed.D., whose passion for education, in its richest sense, and compassion for those he educates, have provided me with a truly educational and transformational experience par excellence.

Much of my professional working experience has been with the catechists, parish catechetical leaders, and ordained ministers with whom I have been privileged to share in educational ministry. They have been a wonderful blessing in my life and it is an honor to work with such "salt of the earth" people. My hope is that this work may be an inspiration to them as they continue to labor in the fields and vineyards.

A good teacher is always willing to learn especially from her/his students. I am beholden to my students who continue in many ways to invite me to grow. Thank you for your inspiration and for sharing your stories with me as you search for the meaning of God and the role of faith traditions in your lives. You will always have a special place in my heart.

My colleagues at Felician College offer an atmosphere of esprit de corps in a Christian Community that nourishes both faculty and students. I am blessed for the opportunity to share with you in the academic fields of Religious Studies and Religious Education.

Thank you to Eleanor Sauers, Ph.D. and Sylvia McGeary, Ph.D. Your friendship and support in both personal and professional matters is so appreciated.

A family is so important in shaping us into becoming who we are. The roles of daughter, sister, wife and mother have provided me with wonderful life experiences. I especially am grateful to my children, to my children's spouses, and to my grandchildren, who continue to lovingly challenge me to help reshape the teaching ministry of the Church.

Finally, I wish to acknowledge my husband, Michael who now shares in the joyful and glorious heavenly banquet with the communion of saints. His love, encouragement, support, and belief in me have been most life-giving to my personal and professional growth. Your spirit continues to enlighten me for which I am so grateful.

Introduction

"Wherever men and women have gathered to tell stories and enact rituals in response to the mystery of life," states Mary C. Boys, "whenever they have searched for truth and sought to do what is good, religious education has been happening. Whether congregated around the fire in a cave, around the dinner table, or in the town square, people have passed on their traditions of faith."[1]

This statement offers us the notion that the process of educating in faith has been a concern for humankind throughout history, and each historical period has brought about its own contributions for handing down traditions and religious meanings. At times, this has been accomplished through systematic and instructive processes. This book is concerned with two such processes, namely, *catechesis* and *religious education* and their contributions to educating in faith. Germaine to this endeavor are the effects of these processes in the contemporary United States.

Regarding the current state of catechesis, on January 7, 2005, Bishop William Skylstad, then president of the Unites States Conference of Catholic Bishops, announced, that on December 16, 2004, the Vatican Congregation for the Clergy awarded a *recognitio* for the *National Directory for Catechesis*.[2] On May 1, 2005, the bishops of the United States published the *National Directory for Catechesis*. The latest publication in the field of catechesis for the Roman Catholic Church in the United States, the *National Directory for Catechesis* joins its predecessors in the family of national and universal catechetical documents that have been promulgated by the bishops of the Roman Catholic Church since the Second Vatican Council.

The new *National Directory for Catechesis* takes a significant place within the history of the Catholic Church and among other ecclesial catechetical documents as it carries out its role in continuing to facilitate the renewal and development of catechesis in the United States. This document intends to contribute to such a task by stating, "This *National Directory for Catechesis* provides the fundamental theological and pastoral principles drawn from the Church's teaching and offers guidelines for the application of those principles within the catechetical mission of the Church in the United States."[3] The implementation of such principles and guidelines is to be done within the context of contemporary issues that surely will influence the catechetical field and the Church as a whole. Likewise, the document is critical in that it may well affect the field of catechesis and the Church in the United States for the next twenty-five to thirty years. Therefore, the catechesis of contemporary Christian disciples, and the next generation within the Roman Catholic Church in the United States, most likely will be shaped by the foundational theology and pedagogical guidelines provided within the *National Directory for Catechesis.* In a word, this is a significant moment in the renewal of catechesis in the United States.

To honor the significance of such a document, it may be beneficial and crucial to determine not only the practical purposes for the document but also to capture the thoughtful message of the writers. For example, the guidelines for *Sharing the Light of Faith: National Catechetical Directory for Catholics of the United States* (1979), were to provide a framework for programs and activities, as well as to foster hope and confidence in catechists.[4] The *National Directory for Catechesis* (2005) follows in the footsteps of its predecessor. The *NDC* states:

> We the bishops of the United States have developed this directory to be a source of inspiration for the new evangelization and for a renewed catechesis in the dioceses and parishes of this country. It is our hope that its publication fires a new energy and a fresh commitment that impels the disciples of this age to hold nothing back and reinvest themselves in catechetical initiatives that ensure the faithful and enthusiastic proclamation of the Gospel.[5]

The terms "inspiration for the new evangelization" and "faithful and enthusiastic proclamation of the Gospel" suggest both a kerygmatic and an evangelizational component to catechesis and so these components and their implications for catechesis are explored within the subsequent chapters.

In contemporary church circles the terms *catechesis* and *religious education* often are used interchangeably. Although the new *National Directory for Catechesis* consistently uses the term *catechesis* to refer to the teaching ministry of the church, some of the bishops, in their commentaries on and explanations of the document, use the term *religious education* interchangeably with *catechesis.*[6] This use of the terms may suggest both similarities and differences between the two. It may surface a tension that could be helpful or detrimental to the perspectives of both catechesis and religious education, to the identities of both, and to their interrelationship.

Interchangeable use of the terms, in reference to the new directory, could suggest that the well-intentioned *NDC* is a conduit for such tension. Such a suggestion could determine that religious education is an "absent partner" within the *National Directory for Catechesis*. This metaphor provides a picture of a situation that reveals an unresolved, recurring tension in the use of terminology that can leave both catechesis and religious education lacking. This common interchangeable use of the terms indicates a need for scholarly analysis of the document. Does the *NDC* leave room for religious education or does it subsume it into its world?

As with any relationship, where one of the partners is absent, it can be beneficial to have the parties meet on mutual ground, and, in the words of Michael Warren, "with the hope of *convergence*."[7] Warren offers a meaning for *convergence*. He states: " . . . *convergence* will mean a taking seriously of one another's perspectives as differing but complementary and a recognition that each has its own special genius by which the other can be enriched."[8] To promote such a dynamic, both parties need to participate in dialogue, in conversation, in order to find mutual ground that would be beneficial for the common good.

However, particular questions need to be asked of the *National Directory for Catechesis* in reference to Warren's insight: Would a convergence of these terms, in light of the document, be beneficial for the catechetical mission of the church in the United States? Does the document make room for a convergence between catechesis and religious education? Should the document make room for such convergence? Is it necessary to do so? Would such a convergence be beneficial and enriching for both catechesis and religious education? Would the implications for the document be enriched if such a process occurred?

In order to find answers to such queries, a forum for conversation and dialogue is needed. Thus the task of this book is to explore these questions within and beyond the context of the most recent catechetical document, the *National Directory for Catechesis*. Through a constructive and critical appraisal of the *NDC*, the proposed partners, *catechesis* and *religious education*, will be brought into conversation within the framework of the document with the hope of creating a partnership between the two for the benefit of the teaching ministry of the Church.

Since the time of the early Church, catechesis has been centrally important. From the mission of Jesus to the apostles: "Go, therefore, and make disciples of all nations . . . teaching them to observe all that I have commanded you,"[9] to such events as ecumenical councils, missionary activity, and particular writings, each era has been influenced by these contributions to catechesis. The Roman Catholic Church in the United States has also been challenged in its own attempt to carry out this mission. As Mary Charles Bryce contends, "The Church in each nation and in each era carries its own particularizing characteristics which assist one in identifying the uniqueness of ecclesial communities in different places."[10] In spite of these differences, the Church has made attempts to uphold its traditions and its teachings. The Catholic Church in the United States is no different.

The pre-Vatican II Roman Catholic Church in the United States had, as a distinguishing feature, the catechizing of an immigrant church. The primary tool of religious instruction was the catechism. The catechetical mission of the church in the United States was carried out and influenced particularly by the emergence of Catholic schools and, for children who attended public schools, by the Confraternity of Christian Doctrine. Children remained the major recipients of catechesis.

The convening of the Second Vatican Council (1962-1965) and the mandates promulgated by its conferees had a major impact on the field of catechetics. The affirmation of a proposal for a catechetical directory, rather than for a universal catechism, was a grand departure from the assumptions that a catechism was a necessary medium for catechesis.[11]

The publication of the *General Catechetical Directory* (1971) was the result of a mandate implemented at Vatican II. It called for a more comprehensive and permeating role for catechesis in the church's life, a role catechesis had known in the early church. The directory also challenged the status quo by privileging adult catechesis as the model and norm, and recognizing the role of the whole Christian community in catechesis.[12]

Developments within the field of catechesis also were significantly influenced by international and national catechetical congresses, where discussions of the objectives and desired projections of catechesis took place. Eventually steps were taken for the initiation of and the preparation for a national catechetical directory for the United States.

In the meantime, major catechesial contributions were made to the Roman Catholic Church in the United States during the 1970's. The U.S. bishops promulgated two small works on catechesis: *To Teach as Jesus Did* (1972) and *Basic Teachings for Catholic Religious Education* (1973). Their major work, the national directory, *Sharing the Light of Faith,* was published in 1979. These works continued to influence the church in the United States in the following decades. *Our Hearts Were Burning Within Us* (1999), the bishops' pastoral plan for adult faith formation in the United States, continued these developments.

The Roman Catholic Church in the United States remains to be influenced by catechetical and ecclesial publications directed to the universal church as well. The various ecclesial documents that were spawned after the 1971 publication of the *General Catechetical Directory* prepared the way for its revision. Such a revision culminated in the publication of the *General Directory for Catechesis* in 1997.

Although the *General Catechetical Directory* (1971) provided the groundwork for revision found in the *General Directory For Catechesis* (1997), the apostolic exhortation of Pope Paul VI, *Evangelii Nuntiandi* (8 December, 1975), and the *Catechism of the Catholic Church* (11 October 1992) specifically provided the theological foundations for the 1997 catechetical directory.

Evangelii Nuntiandi (1975) is noted in the *GDC* for its privileging of evangelization as "an indispensable point of reference for catechesis."[13] *Catechesi Tradendae* (1979), the apostolic exhortation of Pope John Paul II, declares that there can be no separation or opposition between catechesis and evangelization. Catechesis, it propounds, is an important moment in the whole process of evangelization.[14]

The *General Directory for Catechesis* (1997) also recognizes that catechesis and evangelization are needed in order to carry out the primordial mission of the church.[15] This recognition remains a major factor in the development of catechesis.

The Roman Catholic Church in the United States continues to be influenced by catechetical and ecclesial publications that address the "why" and the "who" of catechesis. A catechism, on the other hand, seeks to articulate in a succinct way the "what" of catechesis.[16] In 1992, Pope John Paul II approved the *Catechism of the Catholic Church (CCC).* Since its publication in the United States in 1994, the *CCC* has had significant influence on many aspects of catechesis. It continues to serve as a major resource for the implementation of catechesis in this country.

The Second Vatican Council called for the renewal of catechetics and prescribed the preparation of a directory to deal with the fundamental principles of catechesis. The *General Catechetical Directory* (1971) was the response to the call of the Council. The document also urged bishops' conferences to prepare national directories for the application of catechetical principles and guidelines. *Sharing the Light of Faith* (1979) was a response to the call of the *GCD.*[17] As the *General Directory for Catechesis* (1997) was a revision of the 1971 *Directory,* the *National Directory for Catechesis* (2005) is a revision of *Sharing the Light of Faith* (1979).

Influenced by each of these national and universal catechetical documents, the *National Directory for Catechesis* (2005) takes its place among such documents in church history. It is poised to make its contribution to the renewal of catechesis in the United States in the new millennium.

The field of religious education shares with catechesis the mission of passing on traditions and education in faith. However, each partner has its own distinct history and theories. These histories will be presented as well as the major themes of the *National Directory for Catechesis*: 1) theological underpinnings of the document; 2) the meaning of catechesis; 3) the context of catechesis; 4) the meaning of "maturity in faith"; and 5) methodology in catechetical education in light of the paralleling themes of contemporary religious education.

A presentation of the distinctive histories and the contributions of both religious education and catechesis provide pertinent information in answering the central question: Will catechesis take religious education as a conversation partner on the educational journey? And will religious education return the compliment?

NOTES

1. Mary C. Boys, *Educating in Faith: Maps and Visions*. (Lima, OH: Academic Renewal Press, 1989), 3.

2. United States Conference of Catholic Bishops. Office of Media Relations http://www.usccb.org (accessed January 13, 2005).

3. *National Directory for Catechesis*. (Washington D.C.: USCCB, 2005), no. 72.

4. See the Conclusion section of *Sharing the Light of Faith: National Catechetical Directory for Catholics in the United States*. (Washington: United States Catholic Conference, Department of Education, 1979).

5. *National Directory for Catechesis,* no. 72.

6. See Bishop Donald Wuerl, "A Look Inside the New U.S. Catechetical Directory" in *Origins 34 no. 33* (February 3, 2005): 532.

7. Michael Warren. "Catechesis: An Enriching Category for Religious Education." *Sourcebook for Modern Catechetics,* edited by Michael Warren 379-394 (Winona: Saint Mary's Press, 1983).

8. Warren. "Catechesis: An Enriching Category for Religious Education," 380.

9. The Gospel According to Matthew 28:19-20. *The New American Catholic Bible, Personal Study Edition.* New York: Oxford University Press, 1995.

10. Mary Charles Bryce, OSB. *Pride of Place: The Role of the Bishops in the Development of Catechesis in the United States.* (Washington, D.C.: The Catholic University of America Press, 1984), 2.

11. Michael P. Horan. "Overview of the General Catechetical Directory: Historical Context and Literary Genre". *The Catechetical Documents: A Parish Resource* 3 (Chicago: Liturgy Training Publications, 1996).

12. Bryce, *Pride of Place,* 142.

13. Congregation for the Clergy. *General Directory for Catechesis.* (Libreria Editrice Vaticana, 1997), no. 35.

14. John Paul II. "On Catechesis in Our Time," *The Catechetical Documents: A Parish Resource.* (Chicago: Liturgy Training Publications, 1996), no.18.

15. *General Directory for Catechesis*, no. 23.

16. Michael P. Horan. "Introduction to the *Catechism of the Catholic Church:* On Catechesis, Catechisms and Catechetical Directories" 633 *The Catechetical Documents: A Parish Resource.* (Chicago: Liturgy Training Publications, 1996).

17. *Sharing the Light of Faith,* no. 2.

Chapter One

The Historical Roots and Concepts of Catechesis

INTRODUCTION

Catechesis, for the most part, is a term that applies to the Catholic approach to educating in faith. This chapter is concerned with the historical journey of catechesis and will explore: 1) the historical background of catechesis and its relationship with the cultural, social, and ecclesial history of Catholics in the United States before the Second Vatican Council (1962–1965); 2) The catechetical events of the universal Catholic Church, its catechetical documents, and their impact upon the Church and catechesis in the United States after Vatican II; and 3) a summary of each of the catechetical documents promulgated by the United States bishops since the Second Vatican Council. This presentation of the historical journey of catechesis will enable us to situate the *National Directory for Catechesis* within a framework of historical and contemporary significance.

We begin this chapter with the historical journey of the first partner, catechesis.

THE HISTORICAL JOURNEY OF CATECHESIS

We are reminded from the introduction of this book that since the early Church, catechesis has been centrally important. From the mission of Christ to the apostles, "Go, therefore, and make disciples of all nations . . . teaching them to observe all that I have commanded you,"[1] to such events as ecumenical councils, missionary activity, and particular writings, each era has been influenced by these contributions to catechesis. This tradition continues to influence catechesis in our time. Speaking to the universal Roman Catholic Church in 1996, Pope John Paul II wrote:

> The more the Church, whether on the local or the universal level, gives catechesis priority over other works and undertakings the results of which would be more spectacular, the more she finds in catechesis a strengthening of her internal life as a community of believers and of her external activity as a missionary Church. As the twentieth century draws to a close, the Church is bidden by God and by events—each of them a call from him—to renew her trust in catechetical activity as a prime aspect of her mission.[2]

The Church in the United States also has been challenged in its own attempt to carry out this mission. As Mary Charles Bryce reminds us, "The Church in each nation and in each era carries its own particularizing characteristics which assist one in identifying the uniqueness of ecclesial communities in different places."[3] In spite of these differences, the Church has made attempts to uphold its traditions and its teachings. The Church in the United States is no different. Bryce observes:

> It is in light of the beginning years of a recognized "Church" that one can come to discern the distinguishing features in a Catholic body marked by diversities of national origin, linguistic and cultural differences, and lingering allegiances to respective homelands. As one surveys the nearly two-hundred-year history of the Church's life in this country, one discovers that the principles of adaptation and respect for diverse circumstances have been in many cases hallmarks of catechesis in the U.S. Church.[4]

In a word, catechesis has a rich and diverse history within the mission of the Roman Catholic Church in the United States.

CATECHESIS IN THE UNITED STATES
BEFORE VATICAN II

While all immigrants to the United States brought from their homelands their specific ethnic heritages, Catholics possessed a distinctive religious belief system that set them apart from their Protestant and Jewish neighbors in the New World. However, what Catholics did have in common with the New England Puritans and Jewish immigrants was a zealousness to transmit their culture, traditions, and values to their children and to future generations. The transmission of beliefs and values were carried out in various ways. One particular way a people passed their culture on from generation to generation was through education.[5] The Catholic Church in the United States offered numerous ways (although they were limited compared to contemporary meanings for education) for its members to be formed in the faith.

For Catholics during the 19th century of immigration, the primary institutions of education were family, church, school, college, and publications (i.e. books and newspapers). What all these institutions and agencies had in common was a deliberate attempt to inculcate people in the spirit and meaning of the Catholic religion.[6]

One key agency in the educative activity of the Catholic Church was preaching. It was considered to be an indispensable duty of the clergy and it was highly valued by the people.[7] In addition, another occurrence took hold in the 1790s. This was the emergence of parish missions, or revivals, whose aim was to instruct the faithful and to convert sinners. The popularity of these revivals increased after Pope Leo XII proclaimed a Holy Year in 1825, in the hopes of launching a crusade for spiritual renewal. These revivals sought conversion and the renewal of religion in congregations that might be considered cold and neglectful of their Christian duties. A key focus of the revival was instruction in Catholic doctrine. Jay P. Dolan explains:

> The parish revival was a key component in the church's educational enterprise; for some people it was the primary point of contact with the church; for others it complemented and reinforced what they had already learned. Like the Protestant revival, it reached large numbers of people; aside from the schools, it was the most effective means of religious education that Catholics had.[8]

The Sunday school (later called CCD) was another traditional form of education for Catholics that was then simply called "catechism". Catechism classes were held in Catholic churches every Sunday as part of the usual Sunday schedule. In areas that were without clergy and churches, the catechism class was always a regular feature of the itinerant missionary's visit.[9]

While catechism classes were important, Catholics never developed the Sunday school as Protestants did. The Catholic clergy and canonical women religious were never as serious about the Sunday school as they were about the parochial school. The Sunday school was intended for those children who did not attend the parish school that, at the turn of the century, represented 60 per cent of the children, nationwide.[10]

While the sermon, revival, and catechism class made up the core of educative forms in the early years, newspapers and other media such as books, catechisms and pamphlets existed for and facilitated in passing on the Catholic culture. Nevertheless, the goal of all of the Catholic educative institutions and agencies was to convert the sinner, to revive the faithful, and to instruct the curious so that the Catholic ethos might take root in the soil of the Protestant United States.[11] Catholic books (written by Catholics) held a religious or doctrinal focus that included apologetics, doctrine, and history. However, the most widely circulated book was the catechism.[12] The use of catechisms for the purpose of religious instruction was the primary tool in the religious instruction of an immigrant church.

Catechisms

The origin of the catechism is credited to Martin Luther (1483–1546). "Luther," as Mary Charles Bryce notes, "decided that a small question-and-answer handbook would be an effective instrument for instructing his followers in basic Catholic doctrine. His manuals became widely known and soon came to be recognized by leaders in the Roman Catholic Church as influential vehicles for disseminating reform teachings."[13]

Peter Canisius (1521–1597) wrote the first major catechism for Catholics, and the Council of Trent (1545–1563) ordered the writing of a catechism that was directed toward clergy for their assistance in instructing and preaching. Robert Bellarmine (1542–1621) wrote a catechism at the request of Pope Clement VIII and from then on the question-and-answer handbooks became the accepted way of educating in the faith.[14]

Catechisms were then written for the churches in France, Spain and Ireland. The intention for the catechism was that it be used as a defense against heresy. The apologetic, defensive tone remained a hallmark of catechisms well into the twentieth century.[15] However, in time, some other influential events were taking place that would affect the context and scope of religious instruction. As Bryce notes:

> The movement toward universal schooling and making education available to all children, whether from rich or poor families, those residing in both rural and urban areas, provided a specific focus for catechisms, and soon catechesis came to be considered a ministry specifically directed toward children. Thus by the beginning of the seventeenth century down to the mid-twentieth century, catechesis was identified with (1) the catechism, (2) children, and (3) classrooms. It was a far cry from the more comprehensive concept and practice of catechesis in the early centuries of the Church.[16]

John Carroll (1735–1815), the first Catholic bishop of the United States, wrote the first catechism designed specifically for the religious instruction of children in the United States. As the United States grew, many of the increasing number of bishops appointed to pastor the new territories followed in Carroll's footstep and also authored catechisms for use in their dioceses. Thus, by tracking the educative ministry of the bishops in the United States, one can chart the growth and development of Catholic religious instruction in this country in the period before Vatican II.[17]

The Religious Instruction of an Immigrant Church

A distinguishing feature of the United States Catholic Church, before the Second Vatican Council, was the religious instruction of an immigrant Church. The catechism, as the primary tool for religious instruction, was an important part of the faith life of the growing Catholic population in the United States. Many newcomers, who arrived in the sixteenth, seventeenth, and eighteenth centuries brought along with their prayer books and children's textbooks, their catechisms. Some missionaries responded to the particularities of the newcomers' unfamiliar surroundings by writing catechisms, adapting them to the language and culture of the people.[18]

In 1774 Catholics in the present U.S. were a harassed and discriminated against minority.[19] This status continued through the nineteenth century as the country and Catholic Church within expanded. Bryce notes:

> The issue was one of hostility on the part of their non-Roman Catholic neighbors who possessed an exaggerated fear of papal authority. Tensions mounted gradually as Catholic immigrants increased the nation's population. Concomitantly the fear of many non-Catholics grew as they projected the Church in the image of "essentially a foreign power [Rome] which, if allowed to expand without limitation, would bring to an end the American way of life." These were fears inherited from the sixteenth-century Reformation mentality and nurtured through generations. They became magnified in this country which, ironically enough, fought two wars (1776 and 1812) to establish itself as a free and independent nation, wars in which Catholics and non-Catholics fought side by side against a common enemy.[20]

Under these circumstances, Catholics became more defensive and therefore took an apologetic approach to their own commitment and convictions. This was evident in their instruction and especially in the catechisms.[21]

Various clergy wrote catechisms for the U.S. Church, but there were inconsistencies among such works. By 1827, a call for a "common catechism" that was desirable for all dioceses emerged. However, not until the Third Plenary Council of Baltimore (1884) was progress actually made concerning the matter, and in 1885 " . . . the bishops issued a manual they hoped would be suitable for the widely diversified Catholic population in the country."[22]

The *Baltimore Catechism*

The bishops of the Third Plenary Council dubbed the manual the *Baltimore Catechism*. However the catechism received an unenthusiastic welcome. Theologians criticized its doctrinal weaknesses, while pedagogues critiqued its methodological narrowness and inadequacies. A revision process was initiated in 1935, and the publication of the *Revised Baltimore Catechism* occurred in 1941. The publication of a revised "Number One" catechism for younger children also occurred in that same year.[23]

The writers of the revised catechism were theologians and not pedagogues. Reception of the revised catechism was cool and unenthusiastic like that of its predecessor. As a result, new series of texts, new individual catechisms, and graded religion books that provided student involvement techniques moved into the mainstream of catechetical materials. As Bryce notes:

> A number of these clung to the Baltimore text as a basis. The majority did not. The genuine concern for a good and thorough transmission of Christ's Gospel message stimulated the movement for better religious education instruments, manuals, and aids that would respond to the United States Church's many cultural patterns in a pluralistic society. (It is hard to understand how a single manual could ever serve such a diverse population.)[24]

Two dominant characteristics of the twentieth-century renewal in Christian education among Roman Catholics affected attempts to find more effective methods. First, this renewal signaled a reaction against the spirit of the Counter-Reformation and the inadequacies of the traditional teaching of religion based primarily on the catechism. Second, it showed a degree of openness to the insights and discoveries of educational psychology and represented an attempt to introduce learning theory in religious instruction.[25]

Religious Instruction and the CCD

The Confraternity of Christian Doctrine (CCD) was an organization born in Milan, Italy in 1536, the idea of a young priest, Castello de Castellano. A basic parish-oriented structure, the CCD basically was a lay organization attempting to provide religious education to all, both the young and old, who at that time were normally deprived of such formation.[26]

In the early United States, the status of Catholics shaped the need for the Confraternity of Christian Doctrine. Specifically, the CCD needed to respond to 1) the unsatisfactory conditions for Catholic education that prevailed in the thirteen colonies; and 2) the grave difficulties met by Catholics after the

Revolution while attempting to provide religious training for their children in a new climate of post-colonial pluralism.[27]

By the time of the Third Plenary Council in Baltimore in 1884, an emphasis was placed on the need for Catholic schools to compensate for the deficiencies of the common schools in the area of teaching religion. Moreover, "The councils of Baltimore served to awaken interest in the plight of Catholic youngsters in public schools. This would ultimately lead to an understanding of and acceptance of the Confraternity of Christian Doctrine."[28]

Bishop Edwin O'Hara (1881–1956) helped spark the growth of the CCD in the United States. He had a broad understanding of the subject matter of catechetical instruction. In a 1955 message to Confraternity workers, the then archbishop stated:

> The subject matter of the catechist is scripture and tradition, Bible and catechism. It involves theology and the liturgy, history of the Church, lives of the saints, Christian art, the spirit of the Christian home; the encyclicals of the popes, and all Christian literature. Behold the materials and the tools which you must use in your profession as catechists! . . . the catechism must distinguish carefully," declared the archbishop, "between the function of *proclaiming* the message of Christ and *explaining* it. The warm, soul-stirring revelation of the story of God's love in the salvation of humanity must precede and prepare for reception of the truth for daily living" . . . Thus did the archbishop in his final message to his beloved Confraternity workers not only keep himself abreast of the latest modern catechetics but also made a vitally decisive distinction between the proclamation of God's goodness, of Christ's redemptive love (kerygmatic content), and the explanation (teaching skill and method) of the lessons which must be learned and made part of Christian living.[29]

The Confraternity of Christian Doctrine and the periodic congresses provided a forum and a platform where the bishops, clergy, and others were enabled to emphasize and direct catechesial concerns, priorities, and approaches. The exchange of ideas and the inspiration and encouragement provided, extended far beyond the assembly halls. The CCD looked upon serious study of Scripture and a better understanding and appreciation of the sacramental life and liturgical practice of the Church in light of the culture and environment as valid expressions of Christian living. In addition, the Confraternity encouraged ecumenism as well as openness to the human sciences as guides for realizing human potential and an appreciation for the value of the communications media. In summary, the CCD introduced a new vigor, enthusiasm and even pride in the life of the Church in the United States.[30]

But the CCD was eventually to terminate. According to John M. Quinn, the Confraternity was a victim of its own success. While the national congresses continued for another fifteen years after the death of Edwin O'Hara, they lacked his vision, drive, and strong leadership. Apparently no one in the National Center for Religious Education-CCD seemed to have grasped the importance of the Second Vatican Council and its significance for the catechetical movement. However, in many ways the Confraternity prepared the faithful for reception on the renewal initiated by the Second Vatican Council and spawned many regional and diocesan congresses that continue to today.[31]

THE SECOND VATICAN COUNCIL AND BEYOND

Before the convening of the Second Vatican Council in 1962, the stage had been set for catechetical renewal. In the United States, immediately preceding and subsequent to World War II, a close alliance between the liturgical and catechetical movements was formed. Virgil Michel (1890–1938) is credited with promoting the liturgical revival in the United States. He sensed the need for sound catechesis if the vitality of the Mass and sacraments was to be restored. Other leaders in modern catechetics followed suit, concentrating on catechesis as much as liturgy. The close alliance between the liturgical and catechetical movements continues to be a hallmark of American catechesis.[32]

A convergence of the kerygmatic movement with the catechetical and liturgical movements in Roman Catholicism also had taken place. The common concern of all three movements was to return to Christ as the center of the Christian life and message, and to de-emphasize the accretions of time. Berard Marthaler uses his own words to summarize this concern: "More is required of Christian education than the handing on of shopworn formulas, tired customs, and trite devotions."[33]

In addition to the congresses held in the United States, congresses also had been held in Europe, where thoughts and concerns about catechesis were discussed. United States scholars were kept abreast of the thoughts and findings of European thinkers such as Josef Jungmann (1889–1975) and Johannes Hofinger. Such congresses, as well as the International Study Weeks, helped contribute during the 1950s and 1960s to " . . . a healthy sense of uneasiness with the prevailing practice of catechizing (that) resulted in a mushrooming search for a 'new' catechesis in the large parochial and private schools across the land." [34]

From the time of the Christian Reformation in the sixteenth century, the genre of the catechism was presumed to be the means by which catechists communicated content. The task of compiling and writing a small catechism had remained unfinished at the First Vatican Council (1869–1870). Thus, at the beginning of the Second Vatican Council, Bishop Pierre Lacointe of Beauvais, France, anticipated this concern regarding the unfinished agenda of the previous Council. However, he urged the composition of a catechetical directory. A catechetical directory would " . . . offer directives and guiding principles about the context for catechesis and a variety of catechetical issues aimed at serving a diversity of age groups."[35] Lacointe's proposal suggests a grand departure from the assumptions that a catechism is the necessary medium for catechesis.

After much deliberate consideration, the Vatican II Preparatory Commission came to the conclusion that because of the diverse cultural, environmental and geographical differences of the worldwide Christian communities, a single catechism for the universal Church was not feasible. Instead, the commission affirmed a proposal for a directory. With the intent of better serving the whole Church, such a volume would establish rules and general norms concerned with the goals of catechesis along with the major doctrinal tenets and phrasing of formulas. This proposal received further support when the bishops' document, *Christus Dominus* (1964), prescribed a general directory which would treat "the catechetical education of the Christian people, and should deal with fundamental principles of such education, its organization, and the composition of books on the subject" (no. 44).[36]

In addition, the conciliar document, *Christus Dominus,* made clear that the document on the *Pastoral Office of Bishops* named the bishop principally responsible for overseeing the aims and content of catechesis in a particular diocese. Michael Horan observes:

> This document, when read in light of the documents from Vatican I (the council that preceded Vatican II by some 90 years), signals an advance over that earlier council in its restoration of the ancient Church's understanding of the role of the bishop in catechesis. In light of this advance, it is possible to imagine the freshness of the insight that captured the bishops' imaginations and eventuated in a directory—rather than a catechism—at the Council.[37]

At the conclusion of the Second Vatican Council, it was determined that the Sacred Congregation for the Clergy would implement the mandate. Suggestions, critiques, viewpoints and the written participation of the presidents of episcopal conferences throughout the Catholic world concerning the drafted proposed directory were submitted.

Another important event for promoting the renewal for catechesis was the sixth International Study Week held in Medellin, Colombia in 1968. The gathering at Medellin was important for contemporary catechetics in that it challenged catechesis to come to grips with the political and socio-economic order that shapes the religious attitudes of communities as well as individuals. Following a theme of Vatican II, it asserted that there could not be lasting renewal to catechesis unless there is reform in the Church and society at large. It also asserted that one of the tasks of catechesis is to work for that reform. Those present at Medellin also asked that the *General Catechetical Directory,* which was being written at that time, recognize their deliberations, especially a resolution accepting pluralism as a positive value in catechetical activity. Berard Marthaler notes: "The existence as well as much of the content of Part I of the directory is traceable to Medellin."[38] The Congregation for the Doctrine of the Faith approved the text and so the *Directorium Catechisticum Generale* was formally introduced on June 17, 1971.[39]

The *General Catechetical Directory*

The appearance of the *General Catechetical Directory* heralded a new era in catechesis for the Church. The directory revived some traditional principles and it reintroduced aspects of catechesis that had not received special attention for centuries. It called for a more comprehensive and permeating role for catechesis in the Church's life, a role that catechesis had known in the early Church.[40]

Mary Charles Bryce suggests that the *General Catechetical Directory* proclaimed two outstanding things that challenged the status quo: 1) citing adult catechesis as the model and norm (no. 20) and 2) the responsible role of the Christian community in catechesis is to be aware of itself as a sign of the revelation of God through Christ and that all are to respond to the invitation "to take an active part in the undertaking of projects, in making decisions, and in carrying out what has been decided" (# 107).[41] Bryce further notes:

> The *GCD* clarified the objective of catechesis: "catechesis is . . . that form of ecclesial action which leads both community and individual members of the faithful into maturity of faith" (# 21). This implied the lifelong nature of catechesis in its relation to faith and the continuous process of conversion which is "always present in the dynamics of faith. Catechesis is one means of deepening that faith conversion" (#18, 22). In brief, the objective of catechesis was not knowledge per se but knowledge insofar as it informs faith.[42]

Catechetical Congresses

Following the publication of the *General Catechetical Directory* (1971), both international and national catechetical congresses continued the discussion of the objectives and desired projections of catechesis. In response to these concerns, resolutions were proposed at the International Catecheti-cal Congress held in Rome (1971). These resolutions were grouped into six main areas: 1) The *General Catechetical Directory*: Points for a Commen-tary; 2) Adult Religious Education and the Education of Parents; 3) Forma-tion of Catechists; 4) Sacraments of Initiation; 5) Relationship between Revelation and Experience and between Catechesis and Theology; and 6) Education of Clergy.[43]

The hopeful spirit and enthusiasm that prevailed in Rome continued at the CCD Congress in Miami (1971). It was at this event where Bishop William McManus, the then auxiliary bishop of Chicago, called an unscheduled, off-the-record session with a number of participants to discuss the possibility and importance of initiating steps to produce a national catechetical directory for the United States. Bishop McManus played an important role in the subse-quent planning and composition of the work and guided it to its publication in 1979.[44]

The catechetical events and the outcomes of these events that have taken place since the Second Vatican Council (1962–1965) have affected and con-tinue to affect the concept and ministry of catechesis throughout the universal Church. This is especially true of the decade of the 1970's that produced an era of interest in and the renewal of catechesis at both the parochial and episcopal levels. As Mary Charles Bryce notes with regard to the renewal in Roman Catholic religious education:

> In general, the seventies summarized and climaxed a worldwide movement that had been pulsating in the Church's life for decades at many levels—grass roots and among scholars, pastors, and bishops.[45]

While the parochial school and church-related college did much to shape religious education among Roman Catholics in the contemporary United States, it was the Modern Catechetical Movement of the twentieth century that made the greatest impact. The Movement cut across traditional institu-tional structures, caused the demise of many old assumptions that passed for absolutes, and it spawned a new vision and spirit. It set out to nurture the faith of individuals and communities and as Berard Marthaler notes, it adopted as its guiding vision the Vatican II call to transform Christian faith so that it becomes "living, conscious, and active" in the lives of Christians.[46]

The Modern Catechetical Movement evolved in three phases; 1) it began with a quest to find a more effective method than the one then in use; 2) it gradually evolved into more of a concern with content than method; and, 3) continued and continues to see catechesis broadening its vision to include a variety of educational ministries and instructional strategies.[47]

The Catholic Church in the United States during the 1970's was affected by seven events that marked a special time within the Modern Catechetical Movement. They were 1) the promulgation of the *General Catechetical Directory* (1971); 2) the International Catechetical Congress held in Rome, September 20–25, 1971; 3) the "National Congress of Religious Education" in Miami Beach, Florida, October 27–30, 1971; 4) the publications of *To Teach as Jesus Did* (1972) and 5) *Basic Teachings for Catholic Religious Education* (1973); 6) the 1977 synod, "Catechesis in Our Time," held in Rome, September 29, 1977; and 7) the publication of *Sharing the Light of Faith: National Catechetical Directory for Catholics of the United States* promulgated by the bishops of the U.S. in October, 1979. These events called for advances in catechetical theory and practice in the 1970's. The first, second and sixth events had universal import, while the remaining ones were more specifically related to the United States.[48] Mary Charles Bryce summarizes the events and their impact in the field of catechesis in the 1970's:

> In reflecting on the decade of the 1970's—from the early anticipation of the *General Catechetical Directory* (1971) to the publication of *Sharing the Light of Faith* (1979) along with intervening events and publications—the U.S. bishops could justifiably count the 1970's as a ten-year span rich with major catechesial contributions which could have a lasting influence on the faith life of the people who comprise the Church in the United States.[49]

Since the 1970's, the Church in the United States has continued to publish directories and documents with the intention of positively impacting catechetics/catechesis.

One such document is *Our Hearts Were Burning Within Us: A Pastoral Plan for Adult Faith Formation in the United States* published in 1999. This contemporary document, along with *To Teach as Jesus Did* (1972), and *Sharing the Light of Faith: National Catechetical Directory for Catholics of the United States.* (1979) have had and continue to have a major impact on catechetical renewal and the Church in the U.S. *Basic Teachings for Catholic Religious Education* is different in nature from the other three documents in that it specifically concentrates on doctrinal points considered essential to catechesis.

To Teach as Jesus Did (1972) and *Basic Teachings* (1973) two small works promulgated by the U.S. bishops and *Sharing the Light of Faith* (1979), considered to be a major work by comparison, are testimonies to the growth and development in the catechetical field. Moreover, they continued to influence the church in the United States in the decades that followed. *Our Hearts Were Burning Within Us* (1999), the bishops' pastoral plan for adult faith formation in the United States, provides one example of the influence of these works in continuing catechetical renewal in the post-1970's era. We now turn to a brief overview of these documents.

United States Catechetical Documents Since Vatican II

1. *To Teach As Jesus Did: A Pastoral Message on Catholic Education (1972)*

This was the first pastoral letter offered by the National Conference of Catholic Bishops that was completely devoted to the concerns of Catholic education. The Second Vatican Council's document, the *Declaration on Christian Education (Gravissimum Educationis)* provided a foundation for this pastoral letter. The U.S. bishops at the time were concerned with the ecclesial controversy concerning the future of the foundational educational/catechetical unit of the Church in the United States, namely the Catholic schools.[50] However, Mary Charles Bryce offers an interesting outcome of *TJD*:

> Although it was primarily and explicitly concerned with those agencies and instruments "which are commonly recognized as 'educational'" and aimed at achieving "what are commonly recognized as educational objectives," the pastoral in some ways related more to catechesis than to formal education as it is identified with schooling.[51]

Perhaps the most important contribution of the document is its articulation of the educational mission of the Church:

> The educational mission of the Church is an integrated ministry embracing three interlocking dimensions: the message revealed by God *(didache)* which the Church proclaims; fellowship in the life of the Holy Spirit *(koinonia)*; service to the Christian community and the entire human community *(diakonia)*.[52]

The frequent repetition of these three dimensions provided what Mark Heath called, "a device for unifying the Message and hence the three hold great weight in the theoretical parts of the Message . . . The threefold formula is a priceless and flexible instrument for summarizing the activities and objectives of Christian education."[53]

2. *Basic Teachings for Catholic Religious Education (1973)*

Catechetical documents written in the 1970's expressed recognition of the need to balance the life experience of the learner with the systematic presentation of the Christian message. *Basic Teachings for Catholic Religious Education* (1973) makes clear that doctrinal substance and stability are essential to religious education and necessary for addressing its goals. Thus, this document provides straightforward access to the basic outline of Catholic teaching that can initiate conversation and instruction about key Catholic teaching. Such action is instrumental for the process of faith maturity of all Catholics.[54]

The document also references the *General Catechetical Directory* (1971) for its context while it clarifies the important role of the catechist and the faith community. Many of the footnotes are cited to the documents of the Second Vatican Council. As Jane Regan notes: "At essence, the teachings of Vatican II are not 'new teachings'; they reflect core, basic Catholic teaching expressed anew for this generation. As such, contemporary Catholic catechesis turns to the documents as the primary source of the Church's tradition."[55]

3. *Sharing the Light of Faith: National Catechetical Directory for Catholics in the United States (1979)*

In the same year the *General Catechetical Directory* was published in 1971, the bishops of the United States undertook a major project with the hope of adding more clarity and direction for those who were uncertain about questions related to catechesis. This undertaking was in response to two imperatives: 1) the conviction that such a work was needed—a need recognized by the bishops in 1966 when they sponsored a "source book"; and 2) the acknowledgment that the specific task in applying the principles and declarations prescribed in the *General Catechetical Directory* properly belongs to the various episcopates. This task was to be met by means of national and regional directories.[56]

The project started in 1971 by the U.S. bishops culminated in 1979 with the publication of *Sharing the Light of Faith: National Catechetical Directory for Catholics of the United States.* The text was designed to speak to the pastoral, religious, and socio-cultural needs of Catholics of the time.

Sharing the Light of Faith is a pastoral and practical document that contains norms and guidelines for teaching religion to U.S. Catholics of all ages and circumstances. It was prepared for a wide audience of persons involved in catechesis including parents and guardians, professional and para-professional catechists, religious, deacons, priests, diocesan and parish committees and boards, and writers and publishers of catechetical material.[57]

There are a few factors that made this national directory unique. First, this was the first time in the history of the Catholic Church in the United States that the bishops shared their decision-making authority in matters of catechesis with representatives of the laity, religious and clergy. Second, every Catholic in the United States who so chose was free to participate in its preparation.[58] Anne Marie Mongoven offers some insight:

> *Sharing the Light of Faith* is an unusual if not extraordinary Church document. It is an official document of the National Conference of Catholic Bishops,

but the way in which it was written sets it apart from all other official Church documents. It was written by the Church in the United States for the Church in the United States. It reflects the Church in the United States. It is a mirror into which we can look and see ourselves. It is the Church's present word about itself to itself. It is a word which describes what the Church thinks catechetical ministry is or should be in the Church in the United States today . . . The directory is the only official document in the history of the Church which was written by the people for the people. It is an autobiographical word about ourselves to ourselves. It is not a word about the past. Nor is it a word about the future. It is a word about our present. It tells us a great deal about who we are and where we are now. It is a present word about ourselves . . . The directory, whether we like it or not, is a mirror of the Church in the United States, reflecting back to us our image of ourselves as a catechetical ministry.[59]

The volume consists of eleven chapters in addition to a preface, conclusion, appendices, and index. Outstanding characteristics of the directory are those particular features and strengths that make it unique and point towards its appropriateness for the Church in the United States. These characteristics fall into five categories: 1) the role of the total community in catechesis; 2) delineation of four major tasks of catechesis that are: a) to proclaim Christ's message, b) to participate in efforts to develop and maintain the Christian community, c) to lead people to worship and prayer, and d) to motivate people to serve others; 3) a particular emphasis on social justice as a responsibility of catechesis; 4) adult catechesis as normative and in keeping with the lifelong nature of catechesis, and 5) the ecumenical dimension of catechesis.[60]

Although the directory had some shortcomings, it reflected the marks of plurality, cultural multiplicity, and unity that characterize the episcopal body and the people the bishops represented. As Gabriel Moran notes, "The *National Catechetical Directory* is testimony that the catechetical movement succeeded in penetrating all of the country's dioceses so that most Catholics have been affected by it and many Catholics can speak a catechetical language."[61] Similarly, Mary Charles Bryce remarks " . . . *Sharing the Light of Faith* brought the Church in the United States to a new threshold, not only in terms of catechesis but especially in terms of its own self-awareness as an identifiable witness to Christian presence in the world."[62]

4. Our Hearts Were Burning Within Us: A Pastoral Plan for Adult Faith Formation in the United States (1999)

Michael Warren suggests that the Church in the United States turned a conceptual corner at the millennium by restating the goals of pastoral ministry, particularly catechesis, in vivid and compelling terms. The two documents in particular that disclose the character of this shift are the 1997 *General*

Directory for Catechesis and the U.S. Catholic bishops' 1999 pastoral plan for adult faith formation, *Our Hearts Were Burning Within Us.*[63]

The 1997 *Directory* is a thorough revision of the 1971 *General Catechetical Directory* that was promulgated by the Second Vatican Council's mandated guidelines for communicating the Gospel. The revised *Directory* placed greater emphasis on the local Church's Gospel practice as the primary communicator of the Gospel message. Catechesis now had twin foci: the Gospel and the world. In this context, the *Directory* speaks of a way of being in the world that enabled interpretation from a Gospel perspective. This theme is carried forward by *Our Hearts Were Burning.*[64] As the bishops state in the pastoral concerning the mission to proclaim the Good News of Jesus to all the world:

> The Church's pastoral ministry exists to sustain the work of the Gospel. One way it does this is by nourishing and strengthening lay men and women in their calling and identity as people of faith, as contributors to the life and work of the Church, and as disciples whose mission is to the world. To grow in discipleship throughout life, all believers need and are called to build vibrant parish and diocesan communities of faith and service.[65]

In this pastoral, the writers affirm the need for the development of adult faith formation that was emphasized at Vatican II and carried through in subsequent catechetical documents. This represents a shift from the Church's emphasis on the catechesis of children that was dominant before the Council to an emphasis on the faith formation of adults. As the document notes:

> Such lifelong formation is always needed and must be a priority in the Church's catechetical ministry; moreover, it must "be considered the chief form of catechesis. All the other forms, which are indeed always necessary, are in some way oriented to it. We are well aware that placing ongoing adult faith formation at the forefront of our catechetical planning and activity will mean real change in emphasis and priorities. In refocusing our catechetical priorities, we will all need to discover new ways of thinking and acting that will vigorously renew the faith and strengthen the missionary dynamism of the Church.[66]

The bishops wrote the pastoral for those whom they consider to be their collaborators—those who share with them leadership and responsibility for adult faith formation in parishes, dioceses, and other pastoral settings. The list consists of leaders of various categories: pastors and both professional and non-professional adult formation leaders. The intention of the document was to provide vision and initiatives that would awaken a passion for renewal in adult faith formation. It was the hope of the United States bishops that such an adult faith formation ministry would help the whole Catholic people advance in authentic discipleship and fulfill their baptismal call and mission to grow in the full maturity of Christ (cf. Eph 4:13).[67]

The pastoral consists of the following sections: Introduction: A Renewed Commitment to Adult Faith Formation; Part I: A New Focus on Adult Faith Formation; Part II: Qualities of Mature Adult Faith and Discipleship; Part III: A Plan for Ministry—Goals, Principles, Content, and Approaches for Adult Faith Formation; Part IV: A Plan for Ministry—Organizing for Adult Faith Formation; and Conclusion: Our Hope for the Future.

Our Hearts Were Burning Within Us (1999) is in continuity with previous catechetical documents. It echoes the call found in the introduction of the *General Directory for Catechesis* (1997) for bishops to have a passionate commitment to catechesis and it moves the image of catechesis from one of an activity mostly for children to one for everyone, although mostly for adults.[68]

To Teach As Jesus Did (1972), *Basic Teachings for Catholic Religious Education* (1973), *Sharing the Light of Faith* (1979), and *Our Hearts Were Burning Within Us* (1999) are timely documents that are evidence of and important for the renewal of catechesis in the United States.

I have not attended to the ideological limitations of these documents. This will be taken up in Chapter 3. However, the study of the historical journey of catechesis leaves some preliminary questions concerning its weaknesses. It would be appropriate at this time to briefly raise these general questions.

In particular, we can explore the limitations of catechesis through an early essay of Gabriel Moran. Moran is complimenting to the Modern Catechetical Movement and to the *National Catechetical Directory* (1979) for their contributions to catechesis with the theories, practices, roles, and curricula they offered the field. However, he claims what is limiting the field is: 1) the language of catechesis; and 2) the church's patterns of education.[69]

Catechetics is a Catholic church language that remains alive as long as it has specificity, concreteness, and reference to Catholic practices; in other words, as long as it transmits the traditions of the Catholic faith. However, the problem that exists, according to Moran, is that we all speak at least two languages: the internal language of our religious tradition and the language of our contemporary society. For Moran, the use of biblical, theological, and catechetical language is acceptable when used appropriately. "However," Moran advocates, "religious education must include stepping outside of that language or at least building a bridge to the language of the nonchurch world."[70] If this statement is substantial, then the task is to determine whether modern catechetics can be considered to be true and adequate religious education. Does catechetics take the leap out of its own linguistic parameters in order to relate to the language of the contemporary, secular world, and to the language of other faiths as well? Furthermore, is modern catechetics willing to broaden itself by embracing modern educational processes, or do the meanings of "handing on the faith" and "indoctrination" exist only as the main concerns? Is catechetics capable of being truly religiously educational? If the answers to these questions are negative, further exploration of religious education is needed. For Moran, the new catechetical movement provided fresh ideas for the field but it has had its severe limitations. He elaborates:

> The emergence of the word *catechetics* in American Catholic literature of the late 1950s signified the entrance onto our shores of new theological and educational ideas . . . Looking back on that movement, however, one can see grave inadequacies in both its theology and its educational theory. The theology was a powerful but narrow neoorthodoxy . . . The educational framework was even more severely limited. It seemed to suppose a priest in a pulpit talking to little children or at least to adults being treated like little children.[71]

Religious education is a term that preceded and accompanied *catechetics* in the U.S. However, according to Moran, the word *catechetics* has remained a European import that never took hold in the U.S. - especially outside of Catholic circles. Because of the lack of support by the universities, and support by only a few of the best-minded theorists in the U.S. Catholic church, catechetics remains, he notes, a parish-school-CCD project, thus resulting in a less than vibrant field. "What time has revealed," Moran suggests, "is the need for a more radical restructuring of institutions that would demand involvement of every Christian."[72] In addition, contemporary times reveal that Christianity is facing an ecumenical era that demands a religious understanding worked out in the context of a single world history. The existence of anything called *church* is going to be in question in the near future. Moran concludes:

> An ecumenical era is one in which any organized religion will have difficulty getting a hearing in a world which is doing its religious thing elsewhere. In such a world, no religious group can expect to have members because they were born into its tradition. Any organized religious group will have to be constantly devising means to make its position intelligible to all intelligent and responsible adults. Education thus becomes a central concern of all the members at all times rather than a peripheral task of a few experts who train children . . . The church's educational contribution to the ecumenical era should be to raise the educational level of the whole community by whatever means and to whatever degree possible.[73]

Moran's critique and observations were uttered some 35 years ago. The catechetical community has largely ignored them. However, his critique still challenges and exposes the limits of catechetical theory and practice. In sum, Moran's thesis was and is that religious education cannot be reduced to catechesis.

SUMMARY

This chapter attempted, in presenting the historical part of catechesis, to show how the field has been shaped into what it is today. Subsequent chapters will explore the present state and challenges that face catechesis and its need for a partner in the church's educational mission in the contemporary world.

We turn now to the historical journey of the second partner, *religious education.*

NOTES

1. The Gospel of Matthew 28:19–20 in t*he New American Catholic Bible, Personal Study Edition.* New York: Oxford University Press, 1995.

2. John Paul II, "On Catechesis in Our Time" in *The Catechetical Documents,* (Chicago: Liturgy Training Publications, 1996) n. 15.

3. Mary Charles Bryce, OSB, *Pride of Place: The Role of the Bishops in the Development of Catechesis in the United States.* (Washington, D.C.: The Catholic University of America Press, 1984), 2.

4. Bryce, *Pride of Place,* 5–6.

5. Jay P. Dolan, *The American Catholic Experience: A History from Colonial Times to the Present* (Notre Dame: University of Notre Dame Press, 1992) p. 241.

6. Dolan, *The American Catholic Experience,* 242.

7. Dolan, *The American Catholic Experience,* 245.

8. Dolan, *The American Catholic Experience,* 255.

9. Dolan, *The American Catholic Experience,* 246.

10. Dolan, *The American Catholic Experience,* 255–256.

11. Dolan, *The American Catholic Experience,* 246.

12. Dolan, *The American Catholic Experience,* 247.

13. Bryce, *Pride of Place,* 6.

14. Bryce, *Pride of Place,* 6.

15. Bryce, *Pride of Place,* 6.

16. Bryce, *Pride of Place,* 7.

17. Bryce, *Pride of Place,* 7.

18. Bryce, *Pride of Place,* 7.

19. Bryce, *Pride of Place,* 7.

20. Bryce, *Pride of Place,* 27.

21. Bryce, *Pride of Place,* 28.

22. Bryce, *Pride of Place,* 87.

23. Bryce, *Pride of Place,* 107–109.

24. Mary Charles Bryce, "The Baltimore Catechism—Origin and Reception" in *Sourcebook for Modern Catechetics,* ed. Michael Warren, 144 (Winona: Saint Mary's Press, 1983).

25. Berard Marthaler, "The Modern Catechetical Movement in Roman Catholicism: Issues and Personalities" in *Sourcebook for Modern Catechetics,* ed. Michael Warren, 277 (Winona: St. Mary's Press, 1983).

26. Joseph B. Collins, "The Beginnings of the CCD in Europe and Its Modern Revival" in *Sourcebook for Modern Catechetics,* ed. by Michael Warren, 147 (Winona: Saint Mary's Press, 1983).

27. Joseph B. Collins, "Religious Education and CCD in the United States: Early Years (1902–1935)" in *Sourcebook for Modern Catechetics,* ed. Michael Warren, 159 (Winona: Saint Mary's Press, 1983).

28. Collins, "Religious Education and CCD in the United States: Early Years (1902–1935)" 161–162.

29. Joseph B. Collins, "Bishop O'Hara and a National CCD" in *Sourcebook for Modern Catechetics,* ed. Michael Warren, 189 (Winona: Saint Mary's Press, 1983).

30. Bryce, *Pride of Place,* 114–115.

31. John M. Quinn, "National CCD Congresses Shaped Catechesis in the United States," *The Living Light* 39, no. 4 (2003): 28–45.

32. Marthaler, "The Modern Catechetical Movement in Roman Catholicism," 278–279.

33. Marthaler, "The Modern Catechetical Movement in Roman Catholicism," 278.

34. Bryce, *Pride of Place,* 131–133.

35. Michael P. Horan, "Overview of the General Catechetical Directory: Historical Context and Literary Genre" in *The Catechetical Documents: A Parish Resource, 3* (Chicago: Liturgy Training Publications, 1996).

36. Bryce, *Pride of Place,* 139–140.

37. Horan, "Overview of the General Catechetical Directory: Historical Context and Literary Genre", 2–3.

38. Marthaler, "The Modern Catechetical Movement in Roman Catholicism," 281.

39. Bryce, *Pride of Place,* 140.

40. Bryce, *Pride of Place,* 142.

41. Bryce, *Pride of Place,* 142.

42. Bryce, *Pride of Place,* 142.

43. Bryce, *Pride of Place,* 144.

44. Bryce, *Pride of Place,* 144–145.

45. Bryce, *Pride of Place,* 139.

46. Berard Marthaler, "The Modern Catechetical Movement in Roman Catholicism," 275–276.

47. Marthaler, "The Modern Catechetical Movement in Roman Catholicism," 276.

48. Marthaler, "The Modern Catechetical Movement in Roman Catholicism," 138–139.

49. Marthaler, "The Modern Catechetical Movement in Roman Catholicism," 159.

50. Richard W. Walsh, "Overview of *To Teach As Jesus Did*" in *The Catechetical Documents: A Parish Resource,* 80 (Chicago: Liturgy Training Publications, 1996).

51. Bryce, *Pride of Place,* 146.

52. *To Teach As Jesus Did* in *The Catechetical Documents: A Parish Resource,* no.14, 89 (Chicago: Liturgy Training Publications, 1996).

53. Mark Heath, "To Teach As Jesus Did: A Critique," *The Living Light* 10, no. 2 (1973): 287–288.

54. Jane Regan, "Overview of *Basic Teachings for Catholic Religious Education,*" *The Catechetical Documents: A Parish Resource,* 120 (Chicago: Liturgy Training Publications, 1996).

55. Regan, "Overview of *Basic Teachings for Catholic Religious Education,*" 121.

56. Bryce, *Pride of Place,* 147.

57. John R. Zaums, "Overview of *Sharing the Light of Faith: National Catechetical Directory for Catholics of the United States*" in *The Catechetical Documents: A Parish Resource,* 202 (Chicago: Liturgy Training Publications, 1996).

58. Zaums, "Overview of *Sharing the Light of Faith: National Catechetical Directory for Catholics of the United States,*" 203.

59. Anne Marie Mongoven, "The Directory: A Word for the Present," *The Living Light,* 16 no. 2 (1979): 135–136.

60. Mary Charles Bryce. "*Sharing the Light of Faith:* Catechetical Threshold for the U.S. Church" in *Sourcebook for Modern Catechetics,* ed. Michael Warren, 264–271 (Winona: Saint Mary's Press, 1983).

61. Gabriel Moran, "Catechetics in Context . . . Later Reflections" in *Sourcebook for Modern Catechetics,* ed. Michael Warren, 291 (Winona: Saint Mary's Press, 1983).

62. Bryce, *Pride of Place,* 153.

63. Michael Warren, "A New Priority in Pastoral Ministry," *The Living Light* 37 no. 1 (2000): 6.

64. Warren, "A New Priority in Pastoral Ministry," 7.

65. *Our Hearts Were Burning Within Us: A Pastoral Plan for Adult Faith Formation in the United States.* (Washington: United States Catholic Conference, 1999), 1–2.

66. *Our Hearts Were Burning Within Us,* 3–4.

67. *Our Hearts Were Burning Within Us,* 6–7.

68. Warren, "A New Priority in Pastoral Ministry," 13.

69. Moran, "Catechetics in Context . . . Later Reflections," 291.

70. Moran, "Catechetics in Context . . . Later Reflections," 292.

71. Moran, "Catechetics in Context . . . Later Reflections," 294.

72. Moran, "Catechetics in Context . . . Later Reflections," 294.

73. Moran, "Catechetics in Context . . . Later Reflections," 297–298.

Chapter Two

The Historical Roots and Concepts of Religious Education

INTRODUCTION

Religious Education is a term that has been associated primarily with Protestant forms of educating the faithful. It has secured its own distinctive meaning and position within the history of the United States. This chapter will: 1) explore religious education's historical path in the United States as well as acknowledge some key theorists who have contributed to its formation; and 2) demonstrate the shaping of religious education as it has attempted to adjust to the events of the historical past as well as to the contemporary world.

The journey of religious education in the United States is rooted in Protestant forms of educating the faithful. It evolved into the Religious Education Movement that was originated in an attempt to educate Christians within a modern world. What Mary Boys names the classic expression, *religious education,* evolved as it reacted to and influenced the cultural, sociological, historical, ecclesial and theological situations and humanistic experiences in the United States.

The evolvement of education in the United States began with the establishment of educational institutions by the early colonists. These institutions also served as the milieu for faith education. Familiar with and influenced by European educational institutions, the colonists continued to educate and to transmit their Protestant faith in the new world.

The subsequent centuries in the United States saw a shift in religious life and education with the emergence of religious revivals or awakenings. This evangelical approach to religious experience became the characteristic form of Protestant Christianity in the eighteenth and nineteenth centuries. However, such a form was considered to be a cause for concern by some Protestant clergy. As a result, the concept of *Christian nurture* surfaced as an alternative way for people to enter the Christian community.

However, with the emergence of the Sunday school movement in the nineteenth century, American Protestant education included the principles of evangelical Protestantism where the Bible became the central text of the curriculum. This movement prepared the way for what eventually became known as public school education in the United States.

According to some scholars, the Sunday school model had its limitations. Concerned with its alleged emotionless and ineffective methods for educating in faith, critics of the Sunday school offered their own goals for church education. Such goals provided what would become the liberal underpinnings for the religious education movement that emerged in the twentieth century.

The early twentieth century presented challenges for Protestant churches living within a modern world. The history of modern religious education reflects these challenges within three approximated time periods: 1) From 1903 to 1935, with the existence of the Religious Education Movement; 2) From 1935 to 1965, with the emergence of Protestant neo-orthodoxy and the shift to Christian education; and 3) From 1965 to 1975 when the search for a new meaning of religious education began to take hold.

The emergence of and the convergence of liberal theology, the Social Gospel Movement, and progressive education brought forth the Religious Education Movement in 1903. The goal of the movement was to bring a new approach to the teaching of religion. Approximately from 1903 until 1935, the movement thrived until the emergence of Protestant neo-orthodox theology. This event radically challenged Protestant liberal theology and it greatly impacted Protestant education. During this time period, the effects of neo-orthodox theology and its approach to religious education were evidenced in the subsequent shift of terms from *religious education* to *Christian education*. Eventually, the dominance of theological neo-orthodoxy came to an end. From approximately 1965 to 1975, a pluralism of theologies emerged. These theologies and the development of various approaches to Protestant religious education represented significant modifications for Christian education. In addition, the need to search for a new meaning of the term *religious education* was beginning to emerge.

With such an eventful history, it is important to explore each phase of the historical journey of religious education, since it has influenced and impacted Catholic, Protestant, and Jewish educational institutions in the United States.

THE PROTESTANT INFLUENCE ON COLONIAL AMERICA'S EDUCATIONAL INSTITUTIONS

The sixteenth and seventeenth century colonists in the new world established educational institutions similar to those with which they were familiar in Europe. However, the English colonists established the most successful educational institutions. For the most part, educating in faith in the new colonies was influenced and implemented by Protestants and their Reformation faith. The curricula and rationale of the early schools were religious and moral in essence and content. Biblical literacy was the chief goal of education and the first colonial colleges were established primarily for the training of men for ministry. Charity schools were founded for the education of poor children and Sunday schools and infant schools became part of the Protestant educational effort.[1]

Common schools were established where Protestant religious and moral thought influenced the education of children attending these schools. Educational reformers, such as Horace Mann (1796–1859), convinced many Protestant, political, and business leaders that they should support free public schooling for children of all classes and religions. This support for the common school, that later became known as the public school, was largely due to the denial of public support to schools supported by the Roman Catholic Church.[2] This denial was symptomatic of a conflict that existed between Protestants and Roman Catholics of the time. The common-school movement was rooted in a white, Anglo-Saxon Protestant ideology that was not very tolerant of those outside this cultural milieu. Therefore, for Native American Indians, Blacks, Jews, Catholics, Mormons, and people of other religious heritages, the culture of the common public school was alien and its benefits questionable. This basic conflict between the ideology of the common school and Roman Catholicism led to the development of the Catholic school system.[3]

EVANGELICAL CHRISTIAN EDUCATION

During the eighteenth and nineteenth centuries, there occurred in the United States a number of religious revivals or awakenings that influenced the form of religious life and education among American Protestants. Such events developed in reaction to the formalism and rationalism handed down to the churches by the Enlightenment.[4] John Elias provides a description of this phenomenon:

> Viewed as religious events, religious revivals featured charismatic evangelists calling persons to religious rebirth, conversion, and regeneration through dramatic and emotional preaching. Viewed as social phenomena, these awakenings broadcast charged religious responses to dramatic changes in the culture . . . These early

religious awakenings had a major impact in the development of Christian education in Protestant churches. The awakenings themselves were educational experiences for adults and to a lesser degree for children. In their tent meetings religious
awakenings took to task not only the quality of religious observance but also the
existing educational methods of producing so-called committed Christians. In
addition, the revivals led to the establishment of new educational institutions for
maintaining and fostering the spirit of the religious revival. Revivals eventually
brought about changes in family patterns, reformed school curricula and methods,
and enacted new laws in the churches and society.[5]

Evangelism had become the characteristic form of Protestant Christianity
in the United States. Such form, however, provided cause for concern. What
was questioned was the relative value of education through conversion experiences that appeared to be in opposition to education through nurture in the
home and in church. The value one placed in feelings and reason and their
role in education in faith was a concern as well. However, it was the former
concern that was cause for reaction among Protestants in the United States.
This tension between conversion and nurture in the nineteenth century United
States would provide the background for the emergence of modern religious
education. This background will now be explored.

CHRISTIAN NURTURE IN AMERICAN PROTESTANTISM

The concept of Christian "nurture" in American Protestantism was rooted in
the writings of Horace Bushnell (1802–1876). The popular revivalist conception, in contrast to Bushnell, was that only in adolescence was one able to be
convinced of personal sinfulness; that conviction would lead to making conversion possible, and that would result in entry into the community of faith.
Bushnell argued against this revivalist notion that promulgated the belief
that children had no redemptive significance.[6] He found such a notion to be
constraining as well as alienating from all the hopes and liberties of religion.
The family was central for Bushnell, who believed that parents should nurture their children with a teaching that was compatible with the child's age.
Bushnell was convinced that education properly began with nurture, since
nurture seemed to be grounded upon a heightened awareness of the social
character of Christianity. In his work, *Christian Nurture* (1847, 1967), Bushnell commented critically on what he determined the "extreme individualism"
of the culture. Baptism, he suggested, countered this. He was a proponent of
infant baptism and the inclusion of children as full members of the church.
"The baptism of infants," states Mary C. Boys, "symbolized for Bushnell the
organic unity of the family and served to recognize that the child's growth in
the matrix of parental care was a deeply religious matter." [7]

Bushnell focused on the essence of Christian education. He placed emphasis on the home as the proper center of Christian education. Such education was to take place through a process of growth and not through artificially induced experiences of conversion. He argued that the child's character was largely formed by experiences in the home and he urged parents to be patient with their children when they went through a period of doubt. He also argued that experience, not the transmission of doctrine, was the best foundation for the teaching of religion for children.

Bushnell set out an alternative way for people to enter the Christian community. His thought could be summarized in his famous dictum: "The child is to grow up a Christian and never know himself to be otherwise."[8] The approach was a developmental one toward religious inculturation. Eventually, Horace Bushnell's approach to Christian education won wide acceptance by Protestants—but not in his time. During the nineteenth century, the Sunday school remained the major institute for religious instruction in Protestantism, and the revivalist stress on (emotional) conversion remained dominant.[9]

THE SUNDAY SCHOOL MOVEMENT
IN AMERICAN PROTESTANTISM

The Sunday school was an institution that originated in the Church of England in the latter part of the eighteenth century. In the United States, the Episcopal Church first established Sunday schools for underprivileged children. These schools first taught basic literacy but as more children went to charity schools and then to public schools, the Sunday schools instilled in the young the principles of evangelical Protestantism. In the beginning, the curriculum centered on the classical Reformation catechisms. Later in the century, however, the Bible became the central text.[10] "The focus in these schools," John Elias notes, "was on the study of the Bible while their objective was the conversion of students."[11] Memorization of the biblical texts, that were believed to be divinely inspired, was expected from children. Such an action was considered sufficient for the realization of growth in the Christian faith.

The Sunday school movement in the United States came under the control of the American Sunday School Union in 1824. In the second half of the nineteenth century, the Sunday school movement became international and the Union produced uniform lessons for all children while it also sponsored teacher-training institutes. Graded lessons eventually were published for all grades and the curriculum of the Sunday school focused exclusively on Christian education and on the bible as a book that was used as a reader for children of all ages. Throughout its evolvement from being a school for the poor and working classes to an instrument of evangelical or revivalist Protestantism, the movement encouraged all denominations to take seriously the Christian education of all their members. By presenting a model of a school with teachers, students, curricula, and buildings, the Sunday school prepared the way for the public school in the United States.[12]

In spite of its many achievements, the Sunday school movement still had its critics. Such a person was William Ellery Channing (1780–1842), a Unitarian minister who criticized the Sunday schools for their mechanical teaching and their lifeless way of handing on the faith. John Elias comments:

> In criticizing the Sunday school Channing offered what have clearly come to be recognized as liberal goals for religious education. He criticized the schools "for stamping our minds on the young, making them see with our eyes, giving them information, burdening their memories, imposing outward behavior, rules, and our prejudices." The goals of religious education for Channing were to stir up the minds of the young, to invite them to see with their own eyes, to inspire in them a fervent love of the truth, to quicken the powers of their mind, to prepare them to judge for themselves, and to awaken their consciences to discern what is good.[13]

Such thought, along with other currents moving in the stream at the turn of the century in United States culture, became a major challenge to Sunday school evangelism. Eventually, the convergence of liberal theology, the "social gospel," and the progressive educational movement, flowed into one movement that became known as the Religious Education Movement.

THE RELIGIOUS EDUCATION TERM AND MOVEMENT

The Religious Education Movement emerged from the perceived inadequacies of the Sunday school in dealing with the modern world in the early twentieth century. The movement rejected the evangelical theology, revivalist piety, and education provided by the traditional Sunday school. While the religious education movement did not try to replace the Sunday school, it rather attempted to bring a new approach to the teaching of religion to it.[14]

Symbolized and given concrete shape at the first convention of the Religious Education Association in Chicago in 1903, the Religious Education Movement represented the coming together of several streams of thought. It was at this convention where the modern meaning of the term *religious education* came into existence. Its existence was born out of the convergence of liberal theology, the social gospel, and progressive education as they merged and flowed into one to become the classic expression. We will explore, in turn, each of these streams.

Liberal Theology

"Perhaps" states Mary C. Boys, "liberal theology can be described most simply as a reconciliation of the scientific spirit of the late nineteenth and early twentieth centuries with traditional Christianity."[15] In other words, liberal theology was a rethinking of Christianity in light of science. Founded in Europe, liberal theology had influential proponents in the United States, such as Washington Gladden, Walter Rauschenbush, Langdon Gilkey, and George Albert Coe. Having a great impact on the formation of religious education, liberal theology became a major component in the movement/field.

A new agenda for theology was established by liberalism. The dominant philosophical, scientific, and historical movements of the time contributed to the normative criteria for theological thought. The alteration from the use of ancient texts as a source for normative criteria signified that certain well-established concepts underwent considerable change, if not elimination. Also, a new perspective on the value of Christian life emerged that was grounded in its potential to transform the social order.[16]

Disagreeing with the negative assessment of modernity found in the evangelical churches, liberal theology took the evolutionary viewpoint of the world by: 1) accepting the application of modern historical methods to the study of the Bible; 2) agreeing with the positive assessment of human nature handed down by the Enlightenment; 3) elevating ethics over dogmatics in the Christian life; 4) arguing that Christians were not just to be absorbed with the salvation of individuals but also were to struggle for a more just world; 5) viewing Christian doctrines as historically conditioned attempts to understand the mystery of human life; 6) tending to give humanistic and social interpretation to the traditional Christian teachings on God, humanity, salvation and redemption, Jesus Christ, ethics, the church, revelation and Scripture; and 7) preaching a tolerance for different religious views and discouraging evangelistic and proselytizing efforts.[17]

Liberal theology regarded modernity as entirely compatible with the essence of religion, upholding that there could be harmony between the sacred and secular. Liberals, energized by the metaphor of evolution, looked at the world optimistically. They saw themselves moving slowly but surely from primitive religion.[18]

The proponents of liberalism claimed that it had accommodated itself to the modern world. Langdon Gilkey offers four principle ways that liberalism accomplished this feat: 1) Liberalism proffered a different understanding of religious truth. Truth was no longer to be considered as divinely bestowed propositions but rather as a system of human symbols revealing the mystery and depth of existence. Religious truth, therefore, should not be seen in competition with science or history; 2) Liberalism advanced a notion of Christian doctrine, acknowledging that doctrine was not so much a statement of unchanging validity but as an articulation of the community's understanding for a particular time and place; 3) Concerning Christian life, holiness was seen as not removing oneself from the cares and concerns of this world in preparation for the world to come, but a commitment to a more just world order; and 4) Liberalism supported tolerance for divergent views and accepted the situation of religious pluralism. Christians were to love their neighbors above all else. Proselytizing was discouraged while true evangelism happened by participation in the building of a more just society. According to Gilkey, these basic liberal principles were appropriate for all Christian denominations even if they might have disagreed with other aspects of liberal theology.[19]

Liberal theology's contribution to religious education was to offer a cordial relationship with modernity as well as to shape the five essential components of the new religious education. These components were: 1) A receptivity to "secular" culture, particularly an openness in curricular planning to insights from the arts and sciences; 2) An emphasis upon growth and continuity in the religious life rather than upon conversion and regeneration; 3) A conviction that religious experience bears far more importance than dogma and creeds; 4) A view of the divine inspiring the person from within rather than compelling a person from external authority to obey or be punished; and 5) A willingness to employ the principles of modern biblical criticism.[20]

As a contributor to the new religious education movement, the optimism of liberalism also was joined with the ethical enthusiasm of the "social gospel."

The Social Gospel Movement

The Social Gospel Movement, associated with such supporters as George D. Herran, Walter Rauschenbusch, and Shailer Matthews, was spawned out of a response to the new industrial society, serving as a corrective to the current individualism of the churches.[21] The general characteristics of the movement were: 1) the emphasis on the ethical ideal of the kingdom which is coming about now on earth; 2) the appeal to social reconstruction as the only way to create the conditions within which individuals can realize their potential; 3) The idea of progressive social redemption which defined sin in social terms, but tended to neglect the more pessimistic aspects of sin; 4) the belief in inevitable progress, that God's method of bringing about the kingdom is by gradual growth, recognizing that there is no discontinuity between this world and the next; and 5) the prophetic denunciation of the existing social order without offering much in the way of a practical program of reform.[22]

Liberal theology and the Social Gospel Movement certainly were major components in the Religious Education Movement. However, these ideologies were joined by the distinctive expression of progressive education that profoundly influenced the Religious Education Movement as well.

Progressive Education

Progressivism can be described as a late nineteenth-century movement that sought to extend the myth of the American dream to a nation of immigrants who were struggling with industrialization. Comprised of a humanitarian impulse that was quickened by democratic ideals, progressivism charted a way of reconstructing American society through education. Proponents of progressivism viewed education first and foremost as a way of transforming society. The movement included the formation of the Progressive Education Association in 1919 that functioned as the movement's centerpiece of progressivism. This association had a three-fold theme: 1) social reform; 2) reform through education; and 3) reform of education.[23]

The Progressive Education Movement, according to Kenneth R. Barker, was " . . . a revolt against formalism in schools; it was more a pattern and practice in education than a philosophy."[24] Some of the main features of this new educational practice were: 1) greater freedom for the individual; 2) stress on interest rather than discipline as motivation for the learner; 3) flexible ordering of timetable; 4) encouragement for each child to work at his/her own pace; 5) learning through doing; 6) reaction against teaching as the transmission of information; 7) a greater dependence on the natural maturation process of the child; and 8) a tendency to open the school out to the community.[25] While many theorists made contributions to the Progressive Education Movement, it was the work of John Dewey (1859–1952), and his role in the founding of the Religious Education Association (1903), that was crucial for the emergence of *religious education.*

Dewey's work, *The School and Society,* (1899) contains a reflection, criticism, and synthesis of American educational thought at the turn of the century. For Dewey, democratic faith in common schools is the instrument of reform; all children are to be the recipients of the best ideals schools can provide. He was critical of the standard way of educating that promoted isolation from the struggle for a better life. He believed this method of educating was dominated by a medieval way of learning.[26]

The school, for Dewey, was the leveler of society, manifested by students being inculcated with a spirit of service, while they were provided with instruments for effective self-direction. He argued that schools should be a genuine form of active community life, not just a place set apart for the learning of lessons. He argued that teaching merely for the acquisition of information promoted individualism. This form of teaching countered his belief that schools must be social in orientation in order for students to be taught the processes necessary for the workings of democracy. He believed schools should not merely reflect society, but should improve it. Mary C. Boys notes,

> Dewey devoted himself to fashioning an alternative form of schooling, one in which passivity, mechanical massing of children, and uniformity of curriculum and method were replaced by activity, group participation, and adaptation to the needs of the student. He acknowledged that his cause was revolutionary—not unlike the case of Copernicus. Only, as Dewey saw it, "the child becomes the sun about which the appliances of education revolve; he [she] is the center about which they are organized." Yet Dewey's methodology also simply recognized what already existed in the child—interest in conversation, inquiry, construction, and artistic expression.[27]

The principles that summarize Dewey's educational thoughts can be found in his work, *My Pedagogic Creed* (1897). Education, for Dewey, was religious insofar as it provided the fundamental method of social progress and reform and the most perfect and intimate union of science and art conceivable in human experience. Education was the "supreme art" because it shaped human powers and adapted them to social service. Boys writes: "Dewey believed that the potential of societal reconstruction made the teacher the 'prophet of the true God and usherer in of the true kingdom of God.' His view of the exalted vocation of the teacher rested upon a . . . naturalistic philosophy that regarded belief in the supernatural as a remnant of a more primitive outlook."[28]

Dewey objected to supernaturalism for various reasons. For him, it ruined religion, fostering absolutism, where people settled for security in fixed doctrines rather than risked discovery of truth by way of experimental methods. Second, it distracted people from the realities of life since it focused on an ideal existence. Third, it led to the false dualism of sacred and secular and was all too often grounded in crass ignorance. Fourth, it was incomparable with democracy, because it too often legitimized the authoritarian rule of an elite.[29]

It is debatable whether Dewey was a theist. Since he was enamored of the scientific method, he could not consent to a transcendent God who could not be empirically verified. While he continued to make frequent reference to the "divine," Boys suggests that: " . . . his usage evoked images not of a personal Creator, but of the point at which the ideal became present. His profound commitment to education was a religious act, though not in the theistic sense."[30]

Progressive education contributed to the religious education movement in that it provided religious educators with a drive to use the social sciences and to incorporate psychology into their considerations. It also legitimized their awakening sense of the dual character of education as both a political activity and a religious act.

The union of liberal theology, the social gospel movement, and progressive education gave birth to the term and movement of *religious education*. The merger of these three movements, at the first convention of the Religious Education Association in 1903, represented a break from the past and provided a bridge to new perspectives in educating in faith. At the Third Annual Convention of the Religious Education Association, the conveners stated its threefold purpose: "To inspire the educational forces of our country with the religious ideal; to inspire the religious forces of our country with the educational ideal; and to keep before the public mind the idea of Religious Education and the sense of its need and value."[31]

The idealistic hope of the pioneers of the religious education movement was that the role of all institutions of society that would influence religious education, that is, the home, the school, seminary, associations, social organizations, colleges and universities, be explored and unified in a common educational effort.[32] It was a public and prophetic vision. It represented an educational approach to religion and a religious approach to education. This original vision would provide the energy for a new movement of religious education.

THE TERM: RELIGIOUS EDUCATION

The proponents of the religious education movement sought to synthesize Protestant liberal theology with the elements of the progressive educational theory of John Dewey. The work of one proponent in particular, George Albert Coe, articulated and developed the theories that gave light to the expression *religious education*. Coe is the paradigmatic example of the new meaning of the term *religious education*.

George Albert Coe (1862–1951), an American theologian and professor at Union Theological Seminary, applied this theology to the task of religious education. In his work, *A Social Theory of Religious Education* (1917), Coe conferred on religious education the challenging goal of social reconstruction. Coe was critical of the revivalist approach to Christian education for its individualism, emotionalism, and anti-intellectualism. "In formulating his theory of religious education," states John Elias, "Coe attempted to blend the science of religion, a local and global sense of responsibility, and a philosophy of personalist idealism."[33]

Coe recognized a religious "turning point" in his life when he turned away from a dogmatic method to a scientific method. This recognition energized his commitment to the philosophy and psychology of religion. As a result, Coe believed that the church's emphasis on dramatic transformation ultimately meant the surrender of the care of souls to a process over which it had no control. In contrast, nurture was a process that Coe believed would be more beneficial for the church to direct.[34]

Coe was disillusioned with the established church and he rejected dogma as unscientific. Yet, he argued for the inclusion of the religious dimension of education. Religion, he contended, allows education to properly fulfill its aim of developing the whole child.

Coe maintained that evangelism was "uneducational." He believed that the aim of religious education was misdirected when it centered on: the instruction of children in things Christians ought to know, on the preparation for full membership in the church, on the unfolding of their religious capacities, and on the construction of Christian character. The aim of religious education, he declared, should be the facilitation of "growth of the young toward and into mature and efficient devotion to the democracy of God, and happy self-realization therein."[35]

For Coe, education came alive and realistic through social interaction and through a curriculum comprised of both the Bible and contemporary social issues. He preferred the use of the term "democracy of God" to the biblical term "kingdom of God," the latter being a social order in which the principles of Jesus would be realized. "In using this expression," Elias explains, "Coe made clear that the goal of religious education went beyond individual salvation and the well-being of the church to encompass the reconstruction of society through social welfare, social justice, and a world society. Working for the democracy of God was Coe's way of expressing the traditional doctrine of faith."[36]

Commitment to the social order permeates through Coe's later work, *What is Christian Education?* (1929). In this work, Coe points out the limitations of forms of religious education where the transmission of religious stories and truths predominate. Such forms, for Coe, run the risk of indoctrination and irrelevance. He makes the distinction between transmissive and creative education. This distinction is captured in his foundational question: "Shall the primary purpose of Christian education be to hand on a religion, or to create a new world?"[37]

Since the church had too often failed to incorporate a social vision into its education, the transmissive mode of education prevailed. Therefore, in Coe's judgment, there was a need for creative education in order to relate faith to culture. Mary Boys explains:

> Creative education, in contrast, sought to improve or reconstruct the culture; even when it employed transmissive processes, they were directed toward transformation. Creative education (not to be confused with self-expression) oriented its adherents to the unfinished tasks of the democracy of God. It contained the potential to reform and revitalize the church. Creative education, in fact, might save the church from institutionalism by developing a system of continuous self-criticism. It might counteract denominational introversion, make the church a base of social radicalism, and reduce the membership and wealth of the church. It might also bring a true revival for which so many longed. In short, Coe saw education not simply as a way of transforming society, but also as a powerful means of ecclesial renewal and as a creative, life-giving force.[38]

Coe viewed his commitment to the transformation of the social order as entirely compatible with this devotion to human growth and wholeness. The primary content of religious education poured out from the lives and experiences of students as these were illuminated by the religious tradition of the church. The influence of both liberal theology and progressive education then, helped to form Coe's meaning of religious education. A good summary of his reconstructed meaning of religious education is: "It is the systematic, critical examination and reconstruction of relations between persons, guided by Jesus' assumption that persons are of infinite worth, and by the hypothesis of the existence of God, the Great Valuer of Persons."[39]

Such a definition reveals Coe's embrace of the scientific method, his leaning toward progressivism and personalism, a de-emphasis of Christ's divine character with a focus on his ethical actions, and a reluctance to give credence to a transcendent God as opposed to an immanent God.[40]

Coe's preoccupation with social ethics is indicated in his final book, *What is Religion Doing to Our Consciences?* (1943). Coe is considered the principal proponent of social-cultural approach to religious education although he was joined by other prominent theorists such as, William Clayton Bower, Sophia Lyon Fahs, and Ernest Chave. These advocates of religious education differed from evangelical Christian educators in their treatment of the Bible as God's revelation. For the evangelicals, the Bible as the Word of God alone provided the exclusive content and subject matter for Christian education. In contrast, the Bible was one of a number of resources for religious education, for Coe and the other social-cultural theorists.[41]

Coe disapproved of excessive focus on the Bible. He feared such focus would distract people from reality, and he regarded true worship as seeing life objectively. Actually, the religious education theorists paid little attention to the question of divine revelation, while they focused on human experience. Their emphasis was on growth rather than conversion. Instead, the expressions of nurture, formation, development, and wholeness called to mind an entirely different understanding of a person's relationship with God. The language of sin and guilt nearly fell into disuse. The emotionalism, brought about by the revivals, was countered with rational, analytical discussion.[42]

The religious education theorists were not interested in metaphysical questions and so they showed little enthusiasm for theology. They were committed to reconstruction of the social order, equating education with salvation of the world community. Their aim was the reconstruction of society. "If the theorists made one thing clear," Mary Boys writes critically, "it was their realization that education was indeed a political activity. 'Hidden,' of course, in their curriculum was the uncritical regard for democracy and the arrogant belief that progress was being made steadily; what was not taught (the 'null' curriculum) was traditional Christian doctrine."[43]

The efforts of the religious education movement and the Religious Education Association continued to enjoy their transformational roles in professionalizing the field of religious education. On the tenth anniversary of the movement, Henry F. Cope, the General Secretary, reported that religious education "has become part of our national consciousness."[44] According to Cope, the major advances of the decade made by the religious education movement were: 1) Religious education acquired a new and generally accepted meaning. No longer an ecclesiastical process information system, religious education broadened its scope and concerned itself with the dominant interests and values of life; 2) Religious education shifted its aim and elevated its ideals, turning from an excessive privacy toward the development of positive social competency; 3) Religious education embraced the scientific spirit and incorporated psychological insights on developmental patterns into its programming; 4) Religious education became devotion to a great cause—a truly religious hope and educational idea; and 5) Religious education brought dramatic improvements in specific fields, namely, in methods, textbooks, graded materials, and teacher training.[45]

On the twentieth anniversary of the movement, Cope once again reflected on its progress. He noted that it had moved in two main directions. For Cope: 1) religion and education took religious education more seriously and recognized its scientific basis; and 2) religious education was now acknowledged as a social necessity. Kieran Scott encapsulates Cope's thoughts:

> Religion is now discovered to be intellectually defensible. Religious education is seen as one of the forces uniting the world of thought. It has been part of the professionalization of general education. It has fostered a spirit of criticism and

embraced the educational process. Its progress is that of a movement, under loyalty to the scientific method, to the vision of a just and compassionate social order.[46]

However, by the 1930s, religious education began to lose its standing in Protestant circles. The eventual arrival of the Depression and the experience of both World War I and II were instrumental in the waning of the surging optimism about the possibilities of the human being. In particular, however, the emergence of Protestant neo-orthodox theology presented a serious challenge to the liberal expression of religious education.

PROTESTANT NEO-ORTHODOXY AND
THE SHIFT TO CHRISTIAN EDUCATION

Protestant Neo-Orthodoxy emerged from a theological movement that arose in Europe under the leadership of Karl Barth. Such an event radically challenged Protestant liberal theology. It also had a great impact on Protestant religious education in the United States where the neo-orthodox approach to theology appeared in the work of H. Richard Niebuhr, Reinhold Niebuhr, and Paul Tillich.[47] Mary Boys remarks on the neo-orthodox theologians:

> Deeply sensitive to the divisions of the war-torn world, they judged the liberal enterprise to be tragically naive in its assessment of progress, particularly as imaged in evolutionary ascent, and sought to make reparation for this arrogance in their emphasis on the sinfulness and finitude of the human condition. Moreover, they judged the categories of orthodox thought to be inadequate insofar as they insufficiently reflected the personalist dimension of the encounter of the divine and human. Thus, they promulgated—albeit in new terms—some of the classic themes of the Reformation: biblical faith, transcendence, sinfulness, and the necessity of choice.[48]

Neo-orthodox theologians emphasized the difference between divine and human categories. They provided a reinterpretation of Christianity that both rejected the optimism of the liberals and the defensiveness of the evangelicals, particularly of the fundamentalists.[49]

Neo-orthodoxy, by its acceptance of modern critical approaches to Bible study, distanced itself from Protestant orthodoxy. At the same time, it criticized liberal theology for ignoring fundamental biblical doctrines in its attempt to make Christianity relevant in the modern world. The letters of Paul in the second testament of the bible and the theologies of Martin Luther and Søren Kierkegaard inspired the theology of neo-orthodoxy. Propelling neo-orthodoxy were its characteristics: 1) The appeal to biblical revelation; 2) An emphasis on the transcendence of God; 3) A greater awareness of human sin; 4) A restatement of the doctrine of justification by grace through faith; 5) The recognition of Jesus as the revelation and deed of God; 6) The recognition of the tragic elements in human existence; and 7) An appeal to eschatological hope.[50]

There were reactions to neo-orthodox theology within religious education circles. In 1940, Harrison S. Elliott published the book *Can Religious Education Be Christian?* in which Elliott attempted to confront the challenge neo-orthodox theology presented to the liberal theories of the current religious educationists. According to Elliott, a conflict existed between the theological interpreters, who considered religious education to be theocentric and the religious education theorists, such as Coe, who argued for an anthropocentric starting point. The latter relied first upon psychology and sociology to establish educational foundations. Elliott could not see the possibility of a cordial relationship with neo-orthodoxy and he opted for the standard approach of the religious educators until that time.[51]

"Elliott argued," Kenneth Barker writes, "that a true educational process is denied if it becomes a servant of dogmatism, as neo-orthodoxy suggests. He strongly endorsed the liberal educational ideal that individuals and groups be able to seek their own interpretation of life and destiny without having the search predetermined from the beginning by dogmatic assumptions."[52] Elliott feared that this new theology was simply a veiled attempt at introducing a transmissive theory of church education. For Elliott, the primary aim of such a theory would be to induct people into the same status quo without respecting their freedom to choose. Such an act would hinder their potential to build a new society. The transmissive system would be more restrictive if the heavy injunctions of the authority of the revealing God were used to legitimize the process. Elliott believed such injunctions would eliminate any possibility of challenging such a system.[53]

The following year, H. Shelton Smith authored a book titled, *Faith and Nurture,* in which he addressed the same crisis that Elliott had exposed. However, Smith's conclusion was in total opposition to Elliott's. For Smith, the issue was: "Shall Protestant nurture realign its theological foundations with the newer currents of Christian thought, or shall it resist those currents and merely affirm its faith in traditional liberalism?"[54] While Elliott opted for the latter alternative, Smith emphatically opted for the former alternative in which he professed that religious education proposed by Coe and Elliott was based on philosophical principles rather than on biblical or theological roots. Smith's *Faith and Nurture* was a turning point book in the history of Protestant religious education. "The work," argues John Elias, "was more of a criticism of the liberal or progressive approach to religious education than it was a detailed description of what neo-orthodox religious education would be."[55]

However, Smith's work marked the end of one era and the beginning of a new one. It was a vital moment in the history of religious education. Smith had launched a criticism of the liberal foundations of modern religious education and caused a dramatic shift in the enterprise. Kieran Scott offers the following interpretation:

> He challenged religious educators to reclaim their distinctive Christian roots, insisted on a sharp distinction between the nurturing process within the church and any other educational activity, and sought to ground the enterprise in a neo-orthodox theology. The typical way of interpreting this shift is to say that theorists and practitioners now preferred the term "Christian education" to "religious education." What, in fact, transpired were four things: 1) the church reclaimed and regained control of its education; 2) there was a switch of allegiance and interests toward ministry and Christian nurture; 3) the link between religion and public education was broken; and 4) religious education received a near fatal blow. In the judgment of some, religious education had, in fact, died.[56]

It is the opinion of some that the limits of the past contributed to the state of endangerment and disarray of the religious education movement. Some saw irreconcilable differences between its original vision and the premises and processes of Christian nurture. Others would describe religious education as experiencing an identity crisis. While the initiators of the movement may have offered an important vision, that vision was narrowed by the fact that it was largely white, liberal, and Protestant. Perhaps, most important, the visionaries failed "to grasp a sufficient concrete and comprehensive interpretation of the *religious* and *educational.*[57]

For Gabriel Moran, the religious education movement of circa 1900–1940 was lacking in religious imagery and language. The shift to *Christian education* was an understandable reaction in the context although, according to Moran, the context had changed.[58] The stage, however, was set not only for a shift in terminology but also for a new reshaping of the field.

A study of the International Council of Religious Education, entitled *The Church and Christian Education* (1947), defined the aims and objectives of Christian education and provided the thrust for a new era of interest in theological foundations. This study, in conjunction with the European-inspired Bible Theology Movement (that emphasized the reading of the Bible as the "history of salvation") established the groundwork for the curricula of Christian education.[59]

A new school of theorists emerged preferring the title "Christian" education to "religious" education and Randolph Crump Miller was one of the first writers to take up the challenge of constructing a new basis for Christian education. For Miller, theology was the clue to Christian education. He proposed:

The clue to Christian education is the rediscovery of a relevant theology that will bridge the gap between content and method, providing the background and perspective of Christian truth by which the best methods and content will be used as tools to bring the learners into the right relationship with the living God who is revealed to us in Jesus Christ, using the guidance of parents and the fellowship of life in the church as the environment in which Christian nurture will take place.[60]

At this point, the continuum that the religious education movement had sought to foster between religious education and secular education was broken. The primary concern for participation in the broad cultural life of society was now replaced with a concern to sever the distinctive nurturing process in the church from any other educational activity. Miller stressed that Christian theology is the foundation for Christian education, theory, and practice, in his book, *Education for Christian Living* (1959). While he agreed that the insights of modern science and educational theory are useful in Christian education, he held that such insights were to be used within the framework of Christian truth.[61]

Miller gave clarity to his theory in his later book, *Christian Nurture and the Church* (1961), suggesting: 1) Individuals were to be brought out of their formational environment and then brought into the *koinonia* of the Christian community where they could search for the meaning of existence; and 2) The individual enters into the history of God's people and discovers the gift of new being from faith in Jesus Christ. One gains this new perspective from the redemptive community and the heritage it preserves, and thus enables one to be a Christian in the metropolis.[62]

The quantity of theorists who embraced a neo-orthodox, biblically based understanding of Christian education, continued to increase. One such theorist was D. Campbell Wyckoff whose book, *The Task of Christian Education* (1955), presented his theory that the aim of Christian education was to nurture the Christian life through: 1) the instruction in faith and doctrine; 2) the development of a Christian personality; and 3) the ongoing reconstruction of the Christian community in order to not hinder the Christian growth of individuals within it.[63] For Wyckoff, the desired outcomes of church education would be "intelligent belief, Christian commitment, Christian character, Churchmanship, and a participation in the redemption of the community."[64] Wyckoff further emphasized in *The Gospel and Education* (1959) that his major interest was in curriculum design that emphasized the centrality of the gospel.[65]

Another early contributor to the new theological foundations for a nurture theory was James D. Smart. In his book, *The Teaching Ministry of the Church* (1954), Smart presented a need for a serious rethinking of the foundations, as well as an examination of the fundamental principles, of Christian education.

"His basic assumption," Mary Boys contends, "was that the church's edu-cational program should be a valid continuation of what was done by Jesus with his disciples and the early church. To insert the adjective "Christian" before education meant that whatever was done must be rooted and grounded in the Gospel—a proposal that appeared simple but that had revolutionary implications."[66] Smart's theory that Jesus Christ should be the focal point of the educational program represented a substantial departure from the Coe-Bower-Elliott tradition. He also maintained that it is the whole church that educates and its curriculum must include five aspects: Bible, worship, fellow-ship, history, and the exercise of discipleship.[67]

Smart claimed that, like the ministry of Jesus, there existed within the church a two-fold ministry of the word, that of preaching and of teaching. For Smart, the two functions were inseparable. Kenneth Barker explains: "With-out preaching, teaching lapses into moralism. Without teaching, preaching becomes remote and aloof from people's continued growth in faith."[68]

Smart also rejected any attempt to make "character building" the goal of the church's teaching ministry. For him, such a goal would foster a form of moralism aimed at producing "ordinary Christians." He claimed that a per-son only becomes a Christian through an encounter with the risen Lord and by entering into a new relationship with him. Thus, foundational to Smart's curriculum design, is a Christian anthropology that has as its starting point the true humanity of Jesus Christ. Of importance, for Smart, was the rec-ognition that persons are in relationship to one another and to God. In his acknowledgement of conversion in *Christian education*, Smart rejected both the moralistic approach to conversion of the evangelicals and the liberal view that had no place for sin, repentance, and conversion.

Protestant neo-orthodoxy and the subsequent development of Christian education emerged out of the liberal notion that salvation can be attained through good education. Theology was viewed as the identifying character-istic of *Christian education*. However, during the 1960's, the dominance of theological neo-orthodoxy came to an end when many developments in the world caused the churches to seek out new directions as well. A pluralism of theologies and various approaches to Protestant religious education began to develop.[69] This time also represented the beginning of a significant modifica-tion for Christian education.

While there has not been a dominant theory in Protestant faith education since the 1960's, faith community approaches, faith development approaches, liberation theories, evangelical religious education, and feminist approaches have influenced the field. Theology, while the dominant factor in all these approaches, has been integrated with the social sciences, psychology, and educational theory.[70]

Although the Roman Catholic Church played a very minor—if not minimal—role in the Religious Education Movement between 1903–1940, there has been, since the 1960's, a convergence of Protestant and Catholic educational efforts. The significant theological, biblical, liturgical and educational movements, along with the catechetical movement, have affected both Protestant and Catholic communities. However, each has maintained its own terms for education in faith. The Protestant term *Christian education* has ensued, while Catholics have reclaimed the ancient term *catechetics* for their educational endeavors. These terms, assumed by both parties, have tended to be used synonymously with the term *religious education*. "Most current literature," states Kieran Scott, "tends to reinforce this presumption—in spite of its illogical and unhistorical claim."[71] This comment surfaces a problematic situation in the current identity of *religious education*.

The 1970s ushered in much thought and debate about the nature of the field and the beginning attempts to resolve the confusion that existed. One person who confronted the situation at the time was Gabriel Moran. He proposed:

> The intersection of religion and education should logically be called religious education. Unfortunately, the operative meaning of that term in contexts affected by the Christian church is one that I and many others cannot accept. Despite valiant efforts by teachers, the still functioning meaning of religious education is one that connotes ecclesiastical thought control for children.
>
> The problem has now been compounded by the rise of religious study which in reaction to the churches pretends to total neutrality and scientific objectivity. Religion can no doubt be studied that way and perhaps at times it should be. But that kind of study is not the only possibility for the meeting of religion and education.[72]

Moran, however, in this 1970 break-through essay, advocates a meaning for the term religious education as an activity that is neither proselytization nor antiseptic observation. He states his case succinctly. "I mean a religious education," he writes, "which from the side of education would challenge the quality and purpose of all education; and from the side of religion would challenge existing religious institutions with the test of education."[73] With these sentiments, seminal thoughts for the emergence of a new meaning for religious education were beginning to take hold.

SUMMARY

The chapter traced the historical early stages of religious education in the U.S. The early journey of religious education, rooted in Protestant theology, begins in the colonies of a new nation, is affected by the events of each era, and responds by making contributions to benefit the educational experience of the faithful. This journey continues to this day as a contemporary meaning for the term *religious education* continues to be explored.

We can see from this historical sketch that catechesis and religious education have had their own distinctive histories, assumptions, and prepositions. While they may have overlapped on occasion, they have never collapsed into one. Each has maintained its own voice. Each has insisted on its own distinctive identity.

One might conclude that parallel developments in both fields (catechesis and religious education) were stimulated by reactions to cultural, sociological, historical, ecclesial and theological situations that called for renewal during a particular time in history. These developments have ushered in significant benefits in each arena. Each, however, has also had its limitations. With these thoughts in mind, the development and renewal of both catechesis and religious education is always a work in progress. As the writers of *To Teach As Jesus Did* (1972) remind us:

> The educational mission is not exhausted by any one program or institution. By their complementary functions and cooperative activities all programs and institutions contribute to the present realization of the Church's educational mission. All should remain open to new forms, new programs, new methods which give promise of fuller realization of this mission in the future.[74]

Therefore, if one is to heed the words of the document, one must realize that equally important is the recognition that today's world seeks a reexamination of the present thoughts, theories, and possibilities for the future of the fields. Such a feat is not easily carved out and yet the future depends on such a review. "The task," declares Gabriel Moran, "of constructing a religious education for the future, far from being a vague, boring, and trivial recasting of tired ideas, is a frighteningly large venture. The ideas and words are not at hand; they have to be patiently discovered, refashioned, or invented."[75] The present day calls us to examine the *National Directory for Catechesis* and the contemporary theories in the field of religious education that impact and will continue to affect the ways of educating in religion in the United States. This chapter and the chapter before have merely provided a historical context for this much-needed discussion.

The next chapter is concerned with unveiling the *National Directory for Catechesis*. This most recent catechetical document published in the United States, the *NDC*, reveals the Roman Catholic Church's contemporary meaning of catechesis. In order to understand the contemporary meaning of catechesis, a theoretical analysis of the document will be conducted, including an in-depth study of its major themes. Such a study will reveal the first partner that plays a significant role in the composition of this work.

NOTES

1. John L Elias, *A History of Christian Education: Protestant, Catholic, and Orthodox Perspectives.* (Malabar: Krieger Pub. Co., 2002), 120, 159.
2. Elias, *A History of Christian Education,*160.
3. Jay P. Dolan, *The American Catholic Experience: A History from Colonial Times to the Present* (Notre Dame: University of Notre Dame Press, 1991), 267.
4. Mary C. Boys in *Educating in Faith: Maps and Visions.* (Lima, OH,: Academic Renewal Press, 1989), 39.
5. Elias, *A History of Christian Education,* 160–161.
6. Kenneth R. Barker. *Religious Education, Catechesis, and Freedom.* (Birmingham: Religious Education Pub., 1981), 26.
7. Boys, *Educating in Faith,* 41–42.
8. Horace Bushnell, *Christian Nurture.* (New Haven: Yale University Press, 1967) in Kenneth R. Barker, *Religious Education, Catechesis, and Freedom,* 26.
9. Barker, *Religious Education, Catechesis, and Freedom,* 26.
10. Barker, *Religious Education, Catechesis, and Freedom,* 27.
11. Elias, *A History of Christian Education,*165.
12. Elias, *A History of Christian Education,*166.
13. Elias, *A History of Christian Education,*166.
14. Elias, *A History of Christian Education,*167.
15. Boys, *Educating in Faith,* 45.
16. Boys, *Educating in Faith,* 45.
17. Elias, *A History of Christian Education,*167.
18. Boys, *Educating in Faith,* 45.
19. Boys, *Educating in Faith,* 45.
20. Boys, *Educating in Faith,* 46.
21. Barker, *Religious Education, Catechesis, and Freedom* 28.
20. Barker, *Religious Education, Catechesis, and Freedom* 29.
23. Boys, *Educating in Faith,* 45.
24. Barker, *Religious Education, Catechesis, and Freedom,* 29.
25. Barker, *Religious Education, Catechesis, and Freedom,* 29.
26. Boys, *Educating in Faith,* 47.
21. Boys, *Educating in Faith,* 47–48.
28. Boys, *Educating in Faith,* 48.
29. Boys, *Educating in Faith,* 48.
30. Boys, *Educating in Faith,* 48.
31. *The Aims of Religious Education.* The Proceedings of the Third Annual Convention of the Religious Education Association, Boston (Chicago: Religious Education Association, 1905) in Barker, *Religious Education, Catechesis, and Freedom,* 27.

32. Kieran Scott, "Religious Education and Professional Religious Education: A Conflict of Interest?" *Religious Education Journal* 77 no. 6, (1982): 590.

33. Elias, *A History of Christian Education,* 168.

34. Boys, *Educating in Faith,* 50.

35. George Albert Coe, *A Social Theory of Religious Education.* (New York: Scribner, 1917) in Boys, *Educating in Faith,* 51.

36. Elias, *A History of Christian Education,* 168.

37. George Albert Coe, *What is Christian Education?* (New York: Scribner, 1929) in Boys, *Educating in Faith,* 52.

38. Boys, *Educating in Faith,* 52–53.

39. Coe, *What is Christian Education?* in Boys, *Educating in Faith,* 53.

40. Boys, *Educating in Faith,* 53.

41. Elias, *A History of Christian Education,* 170.

42. Boys, *Educating in Faith,* 57.

43. Boys, *Educating in Faith,* 58.

44. Henry F. Cope, "Ten Years Progress" *Religious Education* 8:2 (June 1913) in Scott, 591.

45. Scott, "Religious Education and Professional Religious Education: A Conflict of Interest?" 591.

46. Scott, "Religious Education and Professional Religious Education: A Conflict of Interest?" 592.

47. Elias, *A History of Christian Education,* 171.

48. Boys, *Educating in Faith,* 67.

49. Boys, *Educating in Faith,* 67.

50. Elias, *A History of Christian Education,* 171.

51. Barker, *Religious Education, Catechesis, and Freedom* 30–31.

52. Barker, *Religious Education, Catechesis, and Freedom* 31.

53. Barker, *Religious Education, Catechesis, and Freedom* 32.

54. H. Shelton Smith, *Faith and Nurture* (New York: Charles Scribner's Sons, 1950) in Barker, *Religious Education, Catechesis, and Freedom,* 32.

55. Elias, *A History of Christian Education,* 172.

56. Scott, "Religious Education and Professional Religious Education: A Conflict of Interest?" 593.

57. Scott, "Religious Education and Professional Religious Education: A Conflict of Interest?" 593.

58. Gabriel Moran, *Interplay: A Theory of Religion and Education* (Winona: St. Mary's Press, 1981), 36.

59. Boys, *Educating in Faith,* p. 71.

60. Randolph Crump Miller, *The Clue to Christian Education* (New York: Scribner, 1950) in Boys, 71.

61. Barker, *Religious Education, Catechesis, and Freedom,* 36.

62. Barker, *Religious Education, Catechesis, and Freedom,* 35.

63. Barker, *Religious Education, Catechesis, and Freedom,* 36.

64. D. Campbell Wyckoff, *The Task of Christian Education* (Philadelphia: The Westminster Press, 1955) in Barker, 36.

65. Barker, *Religious Education, Catechesis, and Freedom*, 36.

66. Boys, *Educating in Faith*, 72.

67. Boys, *Educating in Faith*, 72.

68. Barker, *Religious Education, Catechesis, and Freedom*, 37.

69. Elias, *A History of Christian Education*, 175-176.

70. Elias, *A History of Christian Education*, 176.

71. Scott, "Religious Education and Professional Religious Education: A Conflict of Interest?" 594.

72. Gabriel Moran, "The Intersection of Religion and Education," *Religious Education Journal* LXIX no. 5 (1974): 532.

73. Moran, "The Intersection of Religion and Education," 532.

74. *To Teach As Jesus Did*, no. 152. *The Catechetical Documents: A Parish Resource*, 116 (Chicago: Liturgy Training Publications, 1996).

75. Moran, *Interplay*, 36.

Chapter Three

Unveiling the *National Directory for Catechesis* (2005)

INTRODUCTION

The first partner we will encounter is the new *National Directory for Catechesis (NDC)*. The most recent catechetical document published in the United States, the *NDC* now takes its place among both the universal and national catechetical documents in the Roman Catholic Church. It is expected to be instrumental in the continuation and facilitation of the renewal and development of catechesis in the United States. Therefore, during the forthcoming decades, this first partner will continue to have a momentous role in the faith education/formation of Catholics in the U.S. Such a meaningful task calls for the need to unveil the Church's contemporary thought(s) on catechesis and catechetics through the perspective of this new document.

This chapter will unveil catechesis and catechetics, as presented in the *NDC*, through a critical examination of the directory in terms of its content, its major themes, its strengths and weaknesses, its purpose, its vision, its place within the history of catechetical renewal, and its role in the development of catechesis in the United States. This examination will include the unveiling of the philosophical, theoretical, methodological, and theological insights, and assumptions of the *National Directory for Catechesis.*

The three-fold purpose of the *NDC,* as outlined in its introduction, offers clues as to the nature of the document. The basic purposes of the document are aimed at the orientation and general planning of catechetical activity in the United States. Its stated purposes are: 1) To provide those fundamental theological and pastoral principals drawn from the Church's magisterium and to apply them to the pastoral activity of catechesis; 2) To offer guidelines for the application of those fundamental theological and pastoral principles in this country in order to promote a renewal of catechesis; and 3) To set forth the nature, purpose, object, tasks, basic content, and various methodologies of catechesis.[1]

The *NDC* will be explored through theoretical analysis of its major catechetical themes that infuse the document. These themes include: 1) The meaning and identity of catechesis; 2) the meaning of "maturity in faith"; 3) the context of catechesis; 4) methodology in catechetical education; and 5) the theological foundations of the document. Through this endeavor, the "what," "where," "who," "when," "how," and "why" of catechesis will be addressed.

THE MEANING AND IDENTITY OF CATECHESIS IN THE *NATIONAL DIRECTORY FOR CATECHESIS*

The term *catechesis* is not easily defined. There are varieties of meanings depending upon the sources. The *General Directory For Catechesis* (1997) supports this observation: "The term *catechesis* has undergone a semantic evolution during the twenty centuries of the Church's history."[2] In *Catechesi Tradendae,* the 1979 apostolic exhortation of John Paul II, the term *catechesis* is not so much given a definition as it is described by its heart, object, aim, etc. The *General Directory For Catechesis* (1997) speaks to the nature and character of catechesis, its ends, its tasks, its activity and its ecclesial nature.

The word *catechesis* derives from the Greek verb *katéchein,* "to echo". The etymological meaning of the term *catechesis* includes the following: "to instruct orally;" "to make hear;" "the religious instruction given to a person preparing for Christian baptism or confirmation, typically using a catechism."[3] While the *NDC* concurs with these meanings of *catechesis,* the directory discloses that the meaning of catechesis involves much more than a simple definition.[4]

The Scriptures serve as the resource for the foundation of "what" is to be echoed as well as "who" is to act as the "echoer" in the catechetical process. Jesus' mandate to and commissioning of the apostles to "Go into the whole world and proclaim the gospel to every creature"[5] establishes Jesus as the initiator of catechesis. A subsequent passage determines the apostles' reaction to this mandate after a gospel account of Jesus' ascension, " . . . they went forth and preached everywhere, while the Lord worked with them and confirmed the word through accompanying signs."[6]

In light of the gospel, catechesis is the "echo" of the Word of God and all the faithful followers of Jesus are the "echoers". Jesus calls his followers to proclaim the gospel message everywhere in the world by transmitting this message by means of professing, living, and celebrating the faith in liturgy and prayer. According to the *National Directory for Catechesis*, the principal means by which the faith is handed on is through the processes of *catechesis* and *evangelization.*[7]

The Role of Catechesis within the Church's
Mission of Evangelization

Chapter Two of the *NDC* places catechesis within the church's mission of evangelization. This is in step with a renewed emphasis on evangelization that was encouraged during the Second Vatican Council. Since Vatican II, the significance of evangelization and the implementation of its purpose, principles, and intentions, have prevailed in missionary documents of the Catholic Church.

Pope Paul VI's post-Vatican II apostolic exhortation, *Evangelii Nuntiandi* (1975) notes, "Evangelization is in fact the grace and vocation proper to the Church, her deepest identity. She exists in order to evangelize."[8]

The reawakening of evangelization in the Catholic Church was the motive for Pope John Paul II's call for a "new evangelization," deeming that Christ be proclaimed to all nations.[9] These developments have been instrumental in reshaping the meaning of catechesis and in influencing its processes.

The *General Directory for Catechesis* (1997) describes the nature and purpose of catechesis as "under the umbrella of evangelization." The document positions catechesis within evangelization and its function of informing and forming Christian identity.[10] The *NDC* follows suit. It states: "Catechesis is an indispensable stage in the rich, complex, and dynamic reality of evangelization. It is a remarkable moment in the whole process of evangelization."[11] It would appear then, that evangelization provides for catechesis a comprehensive conceptual framework within which catechesis finds its meaning. Let us first turn, then, to this conceptual framework to disclose the meaning of evangelization.

After the call for the renewal of evangelization that took place during the Second Vatican Council, the topic of evangelization was considered in depth at the 1974 Synod of Bishops. However, the bishops provided no written guidelines for the church. Instead, they chose to encourage Pope Paul VI to reflect on the Synod's discussions and to provide the theological and pastoral direction that was needed. As a result of this urging, Pope Paul VI promulgated the apostolic exhortation *Evangelii Nuntiandi (On Evangelization in the Modern World)* on December 8, 1975.

The promulgation of *Evangelii Nuntiandi* was prompted by a concern particular to catechesis. Catechesis, while recognized as a form of the ministry of the word, also has the task of initiating church members into the meaning of Christian signs and symbols. However, it was acknowledged in Church circles that, too often, parish catechesis is directed toward those who are in need of consciously accepting the gospel proclamation. In other words, the catechizing of persons was to include the recognition of the need for evangelization. This need was to be met by the Church proclaiming, more intentionally and more assertively, the love of God to all—both those outside and those within the Catholic community.[12]

While a broad concept of evangelization is presented in this document, Pope Paul VI names catechetical instruction as an element of evangelization. The document seems, according to Catherine Dooley, to imply a distinction between catechesis and evangelization without dealing explicitly with the relationship between them.[13]

Evangelii Nuntiandi reflected many of the elements found in the kerygmatic movement, particularly the emphasis on preaching the good news of salvation in Jesus Christ. However, the document placed greater stress on the evangelization of cultures, going beyond the kerygmatic movement spearheaded by Josef Jungmann.

Pope John Paul II's apostolic exhortation, *Catechesi Tradendae (CT)* (1979) went beyond Paul VI's reflections in *Evangelii Nuntiandi,* shifting the paradigm, positioning evangelization and catechesis as intimate soul mates. While *CT* names catechesis as a dimension of evangelization, it states: " . . . there is no separation or opposition between catechesis and evangelization. Nor can the two be simply identified with each other. Instead, they have close links whereby they integrate and complement each other."[14]

The ideas presented in *Evangelii Nuntiandi* and *Catechesi Tradendae* were expanded in later writings, under the heading "new evangelization" in Pope John Paul II's encyclical *Redemptoris Missio* (1990). In this document, John Paul II affirms the broad understanding held by Pope Paul VI. He distinguishes three phases of evangelization; 1) *evangelization,* that is a cross-cultural preaching to those peoples who do not yet know Christ and the Gospel; 2) *continuing evangelization,* that is the pastoral care of Christians already committed to the Gospel; and 3) *reevangelization,* that is the proclamation of the Gospel to the unchurched within one's own culture or society and to those who do not practice their faith (*RM,* n. 33).[15]

However, John Paul II's call for a "new evangelization" inspired the *General Directory for Catechesis* (1997) to share the pope's concern about the revitalization of evangelization and its association with catechesis. The descriptive conciliar term for catechesis, "ministry of the word" now was seen in relationship to the ministry of evangelization. The *GDC* supported this blending.

In a similar manner, the *National Directory for Catechesis* speaks of catechesis in relation to evangelization. In the directory, catechesis does not stand alone in communicating the message of salvation. It does so within the context of evangelization.

The Meaning of Evangelization in the National Directory
for Catechesis

The term *evangelization* is from the Greek word *evangelos* meaning " bringing good news." Traditionally, the term, however, is associated with an ecclesial significance: "to convert or seek to convert someone to Christianity."[16]

The bishops in the United States have noted in their strategic document, *Go and Make Disciples* (1992), that the term *evangelization* may, at times, raise uncomfortable images for Catholics in light of the culture of the United States. In this country, according to the document, evangelism sometimes has meant only an individual response to enthusiastic preaching, or a style of mass religion, or contrived ways to recruit new members, or a way to play on people's needs. The United States bishops assert that evangelized people are related to Jesus, accept his Gospel, receive his spirit, and become his disciples. As participants in the church, disciples celebrate God's love in worship, in service to others, and in relationship with the community, that is the church.[17]

The *National Directory for Catechesis* also emphasizes the "new evangelization" of Pope John Paul II. "The new evangelization," it states, "is aimed at personal transformation through the development of a personal relationship with God, participation in sacramental worship, the development of a mature ethical and social conscience, ongoing catechesis, and a deepening integration of faith into all areas of life."[18]

The *NDC* enunciates *Evangelii Nuntiandi* in claiming that the church's evangelizing activity consists of several essential elements: 1) proclaiming Christ; 2) preaching Christ; 3) bearing witness to Christ; 4) teaching Christ; and 5) celebrating Christ's sacraments. These elements of evangelization are activated through a developmental stage process that includes: 1) missionary activity directed toward non-believers or those who live in religious indifference; 2) the initial proclamation of the Gospel; 3) initial catechetical activity for those who choose the Gospel or need to complete their initiation; and 4) pastoral activity directed toward those of mature Christian faith.[19]

These elements of evangelization are aimed at both the interior change of individuals and the external change of societies.[20]

In order to revitalize the church's response to Pope John Paul's call for a "new evangelization," the *NDC* offers pastoral directives for evangelization. These directives are offered to all parishes and dioceses in the United States so they might integrate them into their missions. These objectives are: 1) to foster in the heart of every believer an experience of personal conversion to Jesus Christ that leads to a personal renewal and greater participation in the Christian life in the Church, the Mystical Body of Christ; 2) to encourage a greater knowledge of the Holy Scriptures and sacred tradition of the Church; 3) to focus their efforts and resources on the conversion and renewal of every parish, especially through the implementation of the Rite of Christian Initiation of Adults; 4) to rededicate themselves to a liturgical renewal that develops a greater appreciation for the presence and power of Christ in the word of God and the sacraments of the Church, especially the Eucharist each Sunday; 5) to make the evangelical and social justice dimensions of the Sunday Eucharist more explicit; 6) to call their people to a more effective integration of daily prayer in their lives, especially the ancient practice of praying the Psalms and the Church's Liturgy of the Hours, contemplation of the mysteries of the life of Christ through the Rosary, and a greater reverence of the Eucharist through adoration of the Blessed Sacrament; and 7) to ensure that all Catholic institutions, especially parishes, are accessible and welcoming to all. The *NDC* offers these directives to give catechesis a missionary dynamic that encourages the continuation of evangelizing the culture, affirming what is compatible with the Catholic faith and challenging what is not.[21]

The emphasis the *National Directory for Catechesis* places on evangelization is broader than its predecessor, *Sharing the Light of Faith* (1979). If the *NDC* is a symbol of contemporary church teaching, then, it is evident that the focus on evangelization has been reawakened, embraced, and permeated in the Church. The Church's catechetical endeavors reflect this as well. Akin to the *General Directory for Catechesis* (1997), the new *National Directory for Catechesis* places catechesis under the umbrella of evangelization, "within the Church's mission of evangelization."[22] Thus, catechesis, in our considerations, will be "set within the context of evangelization."[23]

Catechesis in the *National Directory for Catechesis*

Aligning itself with the *General Directory for Catechesis* (1997) and *Catechesi Tradendae* (1979), the new *National Directory for Catechesis* interprets catechesis as a ministry that is "an essential moment in the church's mission of evangelization."[24] The new document views this missionary concept and specifically names catechesis "as a fundamental ecclesial service to the church in the United States."[25]

Echoing past catechetical documents, the *NDC* describes catechesis as holding a place of central importance within the Catholic Church's mission of evangelization. In other words, without catechesis, faith would not mature, education in the faith would not transpire, and discipleship in Jesus would not be fostered. The aim of catechesis, therefore, is the teaching and maturation stage within the whole process of evangelization. While the

Church's evangelizing activity consists of proclaiming, preaching, bearing witness to, teaching, and celebrating Christ for the purpose of personal, interior and societal change and/or conversion, [26] it is catechesis that matures initial conversion to make it into a living, explicit, and fruitful confession of faith.[27]

The directory emphasizes how catechesis accomplishes this task:

> Catechesis nurtures the seed of faith sown by the Holy Spirit through the initial proclamation of the Gospel. It gives growth to the gift of faith given in Baptism and elaborates the meaning of the sacraments. Catechesis develops a deeper understanding of the mystery of Christ, encourages more profound incorporation into the Church, and nourishes Christian living. It encourages discipleship in Christ and instructs in Christian prayer. Just as the mission of evangelization enlivens the Church's pastoral and missionary activity, catechesis makes concrete her mission of evangelization. It constitutes the "good news" that Christ commissioned his apostles to spread throughout the whole world and announce to every person.[28]

Catechesis takes its place within the evangelization process as it joins the stages/dimensions of pre-evangelization and missionary preaching with the following: 1) initiatory catechesis; 2) mystagogical or post-baptismal catechesis; 3) permanent or continuing catechesis; 4) liturgical catechesis; and 5) theological catechesis.[29] The *National Directory for Catechesis* ensures that these stages are not separated from one another. The specific stages/dimensions of catechesis will be treated later in this chapter.

While the directory links the meaning of catechesis with the meaning of evangelization, it does give attention to the characteristics that are specific to catechesis. These include: 1) the source and sources of catechesis; and 2) the nature and purpose of catechesis. The *NDC* provides the principles of these features. The following is a brief summary of each:

1) The Source and Sources of Catechesis—The directory determines that the pivotal source of catechesis is the word of God that is revealed by Jesus Christ. The content of catechesis will always be drawn from the church's sacred tradition (the transmission of the word of God that has been entrusted to the apostles of Jesus and the Holy Spirit) and Sacred Scripture (the word of God based on the thought, spirit, and perspective of the Old and New Testaments).

   Secondary sources of catechesis that enrich and enliven catechesis, making it more fruitful are: a) the celebration of the liturgy, b) a theology that seeks the fuller understanding of the Gospel message, c) the Word of God alive and witnessed in the lives of the saints and the Christian faithful, and d) the genuine moral values that make known the Word of God.

2) The Nature and Purpose of Catechesis—Catechesis is the particular form of the ministry of the word whose aim is to bring about in the believer "an ever more mature faith in Jesus Christ, a deeper knowledge and love of his person and message, and a firm commitment to follow him."[30]

   a) The Object of Catechesis—is communion with Jesus Christ. Jesus is at the heart of catechesis[31] and so catechesis is to lead people to enter the mystery of Christ, to encounter him, and to discover themselves and the meaning of their lives.

   b) Catechesis and the Church—Catechesis provides a fundamental dimension to the church's pastoral activity. It gives form to missionary preaching that assists in the early examination of reasons for belief, communicates the essential elements in the experience of Christian living, prepares for the celebration of the sacraments, instills a zeal for the unity of Christians, and prepares one for the ecumenical understanding and mission of the Church.

   As the origin, locus, and goal of catechesis, the Church provides the historical foundation, primary setting, and the goal for catechesis, which is to build up the Body of Christ, the Church. Therefore, "'Catechesis is an essentially ecclesial act'—an action of the Church." [32]

Both initiatory catechesis and ongoing catechesis, noted within the nature and purpose of catechesis, will be treated further in the "Maturity in Faith" section of this chapter.

The Tasks of Catechesis

Since the fundamental task of catechesis is the formation of disciples of Jesus Christ, catechesis must attend to the different dimensions of faith. Each of these dimensions becomes a distinct yet complementary task. Catechesis comprises six fundamental tasks.[33] These tasks are:

a) Catechesis promotes knowledge of the faith—The knowledge of faith emerges from the content of God's self-revelation that is found in Sacred Scripture, Sacred Tradition, and to the doctrinal formulas found in the Creeds.

b) Catechesis promotes knowledge of the meaning of the Liturgy and the sacraments—Through the liturgical celebrations of the Church, the believer comes to know Christ since he is present in the sacraments. The promotion of an active and conscious participation in the liturgy of the church is aided by forming the minds of the faithful for prayer, for thanksgiving, for repentance, for praying with confidence, for a community spirit, and for understanding correctly the meaning of the creeds.[34]

c) Catechesis promotes moral formation in Jesus Christ—The aim of moral catechesis is to conform the believer to Christ in order to bring about personal transformation and conversion. Therefore, catechesis must transmit the content of Christ's moral teachings as well as their implications for Christian living. The faithful should be encouraged to give witness to Christ's teaching in their private lives and in the public arena, thus demonstrating the social consequences of the demands of the Gospel.[35]

d) Catechesis teaches the Christian how to pray with Christ—Those who are converted to Christ and are in communion with him are led to adopt his disposition of prayer and reflection. Therefore, all catechesis should provide a prayerful environment.

e) Catechesis prepares the Christian to live in community and to participate actively in the life and mission of the Church—The basis for the disciples' life in community is Jesus' greatest commandment, that is, to love one another. "Catechesis encourages an apprenticeship in Christian living that is based on Christ's teachings about community life."[36]

f) Catechesis promotes a missionary spirit that prepares the faithful to be present as Christians in society—As a member of society, the disciple is to fulfill her/his Christian duty by bearing witness to faith in words and deeds. Catechesis seeks to help the disciple by nourishing the evangelical attitudes of Jesus Christ in the faithful. It encourages adherents of the world's religions to share what they hold in common, never minimizing the real differences between and among them."[37]

In order for catechesis to accomplish its goal of attaining the formation and full development of Jesus' disciples, these six tasks are to be realized as a unified whole. Each task recognizes the object of catechesis and each is interdependent with the other tasks. The transmission of the gospel message and the experience of the Christian life are needed for catechesis to accomplish these tasks.[38]

As noted, the meaning of catechesis in the Directory consistently is blended within the meaning of evangelization. The *NDC* claims that while catechesis and evangelization cannot be simply identified with one another, there is no separation or opposition between them; they integrate and complement each other.[39] In other words, they are wedded to one another.

Catechesis and evangelization then, are inseparable. Does this union signify that the terms *catechesis* and *evangelization* should ever be separated in the usage and description of their tasks? The directory continually distinguishes the terms, yet it acknowledges their common mission. If catechesis is an *evangelizing catechesis*, then, should that not be the term of choice? Catherine Dooley notes that the papal and episcopal documents promulgated since the Second Vatican Council call for an explicit partnership in the new millenium: "they call for an *evangelizing catechesis*."[40] Dooley predicts that the term, used by Johannes Hofinger, will take on a new connotation for the twenty-first century.[41] If Dooley's prediction is true, then why does the first catechetical document of the twenty-first century not utilize the term? Rather, catechesis is placed within the mission of evangelization. Does catechesis lose some of its own meaning and identity when it is perceived only through the meaning and identity of evangelization? Does positioning the meaning of catechesis only within the context of evangelization prevent catechesis from growing and developing into something more than it is or can be? And, what of its relationship to religious education?

THE MEANING OF "MATURITY IN FAITH"
IN THE *NATIONAL DIRECTORY FOR CATECHESIS*

"And he gave some as apostles, others as prophets, others as evangelists, others as pastors and teachers, to equip the holy ones for the work of ministry, for building up the body of Christ, until we all attain to the unity of faith and knowledge of the Son of God, to mature manhood [personhood], to the extent of the full stature of Christ . . . ."[42] This passage from St. Paul's letter to the Ephesians presents an image that can be related to contemporary catechesis. The notion of mature personhood or *maturity in faith* has been developed particularly in the catechetical field within approximately the last fifty years.[43]

Maturity in faith was not a new catechetical theme at the Second Vatican Council. The French school of catechetics had popularized it during the 1950's and 1960's. The theme was a logical outcome of the developmental approach. "Scripture and tradition were cited to show," Berard Marthaler states, "that faith cannot be reduced to a static reality like a deposit in a bank vault which one preserves by secrecy and surveillance."[44] In other words, the profession of faith is not to be isolated from the context of everyday living but is to be seen as a complex, dynamic force. The French authors argued the need for catechesis to relate faith to the process of growth and maturation of individuals and groups if men and women are to become truly adult Christians.[45] This need was recognized at the Second Vatican Council (1962–1965) and it continued and continues to be developed in the subsequent and contemporary catechetical directories and documents.

The *General Catechetical Directory* (1971), in its particular genre, laid the foundation for the importance of mature faith and the role of catechesis in the process. It states: " . . . catechesis is the term to be used for that form of ecclesial action which leads both communities and individual members of the faithful to maturity of faith."[46] The directory emphasized that as the human person develops in stages toward maturity, faith also is developed through the various stages of one's life. A function of catechesis is to lend aid for the beginning and the developmental process of faith throughout the course of a person's existence. The explanation and application of the revelation of truth to one's life is instrumental to one's development of faith.[47] In the United States, the meaning and implications of the term *maturity in faith* culminated in the bishops' pastoral document, *Our Hearts Were Burning Within Us* (1999).

The *National Directory for Catechesis* also recognizes maturity in faith and the development of faith, particularly in Chapter 7, "Catechizing the People of God in Diverse Settings." We now turn our attention to this recognition in the *NDC*.

Maturity in Faith

We are reminded in Chapter 2 of the *National Directory for Catechesis* that for the believer, catechesis: 1) matures initial conversion to make it into a living, explicit, and fruitful confession of faith; and 2) aims to bring about a mature faith in Jesus Christ. As the teaching and maturation stage within the process of evangelization, catechesis is to bring about in the Christian a deeper knowledge and love of Jesus Christ and a firm commitment to follow him. The mature Christian, according to the *NDC,* is one who has 1) accepted by faith the person of Jesus Christ as the one Lord; 2) has given him complete adherence by sincere conversion of heart; 3) endeavors to know better this Jesus to whom he has entrusted himself; 4) to know his 'mystery,' the Kingdom of God proclaimed by him, the requirements and promises contained in his Gospel message; and 5) knowledge of the paths that Jesus has laid down for any one who wishes to follow him.[48]

While all the baptized are called by God to maturity of faith,[49] it is, according to the *NDC,* adult persons who are "capable of a free and informed response of faith to God's initiative of love" and who "have experienced the joys and challenges of life and have the capacity to question the truth and meaning of life."[50] Therefore, it would be significant to examine further what the directory offers in its perspective of the adult and in its meaning of catechesis for the adult.

The Adult and Catechesis

The *National Directory for Catechesis* emphasizes the importance of the adult and the catechesis of adults. In what appears to be a symbolic gesture, the directory departs from its predecessor, *Sharing the Light of Faith* (1979) in laying out the stages of life in relation to catechesis. *Sharing the Light of Faith* begins with the catechesis of infants/children and in ascending order, concludes with the catechesis of adults. The *National Directory for Catechesis* begins with the catechesis of adults and descends to the catechesis of infants/children. This represents a shift in church thought from the emphasis of catechesis for children to adult catechesis as the principal form of catechesis. The *NDC* states,

> "The catechesis of adults . . . is the principal form of catechesis, because it is addressed to persons who have the greatest responsibilities and the capacity to live the Christian message in its fully developed form." The catechetical formation of adults is essential for the Church to carry out the commission given the apostles by Christ. 'Because of its importance and because all other forms of catechesis are oriented in some way to it, the catechesis of adults must have high priority at all levels of the Church.'"[51]

In providing a "comprehensive and systematic presentation and exploration of the core elements of Catholic faith and practice—a complete initiation into a Catholic way of life,"[52] adult catechesis endeavors to attain its goals. These goals are: 1) to invite and enable adults to an attitude of conversion; 2) to help adults make a conscious and firm decision to live the gift and choice of faith through membership in the Christian community; and 3) to help adults become more willing and able to be Christian disciples in the world.[53] These goals are to be manifested through tasks that are particular to adult catechesis. These tasks are: 1) to promote formation and development of life in the Risen Christ through the sacraments, prayer life of the Church, works of charity and justice, retreats, and spiritual direction; 2) to promote evangelization as the means of bringing the Good News to all states of humanity; 3) to educate toward the development of an informed moral conscience; 4) to clarify religious and moral questions; 5) to clarify the relationship between the Church and the world, especially in light of the church's social doctrine; 6) to develop the rational foundations of the faith and demonstrate the compatibility of faith and reason; 7) to encourage adults to assume their baptismal responsibility for the church's mission and to be able to give Christian witness in society; and 8) to develop creative ways to interest and encourage adults to take advantage of the various programs of enrichment and spiritual development being offered.[54]

Adult catechesis is to be cognitive, experiential, and behavioral. Acknowledging that Sacred Scripture and tradition form the basic content for adult catechesis, the directory promotes the *Catechism of the Catholic Church* (1997) as the normative reference text for adult catechesis. The distinct, yet complementary, aspects of the Catholic faith, according to the directory, provide a dimension for Christian discipleship and maturity in faith. In this regard, the directory quotes the *General Directory of Catechesis* (1997): "The maturation of the Christian life requires that it be cultivated in all its dimensions: knowledge of the faith, liturgical life, moral formation, prayer, belonging to community, missionary spirit. When catechesis omits one of these elements, the Christian faith does not attain full development."[55] Therefore, the *NDC* notes, adult catechesis should include: 1) study of Sacred Scripture and tradition, the creeds and doctrines of the faith, the hierarchy of truths, and the history of the Church; 2) study of the Mass, the sacraments, and the daily prayer life of the Church; 3) a focus on the universal call to holiness, including a study of the Ten Commandments, the Beatitudes, and Jesus' commandment to love one another as he has loved us; 4) The Church's teaching on the dignity of the human person, sin, grace, the virtues, and conscience formation; 5) the Church's social teachings and the implications of social sin; 6) prayer and the various traditions of spirituality within Catholicism; 7) the structure and authority of the Church and the rights and responsibilities of the baptized; 8) marriage and family life, single life; 9) the ecumenical movement and inter-religious dialogue; and 10) the Church's mission in the world and for the world, and the nature of the lay apostolate.[56]

The directory upholds that whatever methodology is used for adult catechesis, the methodology always is to ensue "a basic organic formation in the faith that includes a serious study of Christian doctrine integrated with formation in Christian living. Effective adult catechesis relates the content of the faith to life experience. It enables the Christian to read the signs of the times in light of the Gospel."[57] In addition, the *NDC* suggests that adults are responsible for identifying their catechetical needs. This would help to develop catechetical objectives in the design of a catechetical plan since "adults have a right and a duty to bring to maturity the seed of faith sown in them by God."[58]

The Directory establishes that every ecclesial community must provide ongoing, systematic catechetical courses for all adults. These special forms include catechesis for: 1) Christian initiation as set forth in the *Rite of Christian Initiation of Adults;* 2) parents; 3) the liturgical year; 4) missionary intention; 5) formation of catechists and those involved in the lay apostolate in the world; 6) formation of Catholic school teachers; 7) special moments in and experiences of life; 8) the use of leisure time, holidays, travel, and pilgrimage; and 9) special events in the life of the church and society.[59]

While adult catechesis is of prime importance and concern for the teaching ministry of the church, it needs to recognize that stages of faith development can differ among adults. Actually, growth in faith toward maturity in faith affects the faithful at various age levels and conditions in its entirety. Therefore, catechesis' purpose is to promote mature adult faith for all, recognizing that catechesis is a life-long process. Such a process needs to be available and relative to all members of the faith community. Two forms of catechesis recognize the diverse catechetical needs of the faithful. These forms are presented in the directory as 1) initiatory and 2) ongoing catechesis.

Initiatory and Ongoing Catechesis

While it is the intention of catechesis to promote and mature initial conversion, educate persons in the faith, and incorporate them into the life of the Christian community, catechesis often must take the form of primary proclamation of the Gospel. This form is needed, since, according to the *NDC,* many who present themselves for catechesis have not yet experienced conversion to Jesus Christ. In order for catechesis to fulfill its proper task of education in the faith, some level of conversion is necessary on behalf of the catechized.[60]

Whatever the situation, catechesis serves an initiatory purpose as it seeks to foster the catechumen's initial faith in the person of Jesus Christ, leading to a genuine profession of faith. This profession of faith forms the link between catechesis and the sacraments of initiation. The directory names this form of catechesis as *initiatory catechesis.* This form of catechesis: 1) presents Catholic teaching in its entirety; 2) enlightens faith; 3) directs the heart toward God; 4) fosters participation in the liturgy; 5) inspires apostolic activity; and 6) nurtures a life completely in accord with the spirit of Jesus Christ.[61]

Catechesis that is initiatory is a comprehensive and systematic formation in faith. It is an apprenticeship of the entire Christian life. The *NDC* states: "Initiatory catechesis cultivates the roots of faith, nurtures a distinctively Christian spiritual life, and prepares the person to be nourished at the table of the Eucharist and in the ordinary life of the Christian community . . . The richness of this initiatory catechesis should serve to inspire other forms of catechesis."[62]

Catechesis that serves the continuing conversion and ongoing formation of those who have been initiated in the faith is termed in the Directory as *ongoing catechesis.* A responsibility of the whole Catholic community, ongoing catechesis fosters the growth of a more mature faith in the members of the community. Ongoing catechesis is a lifelong process whose aim is to make each person's faith living, explicit, active, and enlightened by doctrine.[63] Lifelong catechesis is to involve: 1) the study and praying of Sacred Scripture; 2) a systematic catechesis that gradually leads people deeper into their relationship with Jesus because they grow in their understanding of who he is and what he has done for us; 3) liturgical and sacramental catechesis; 4) initiatives of spiritual formation; and 5) thorough examination of the church's social teachings.[64]

Growth in Faith Toward a Maturity in Faith

"Growth in faith," the *NDC* states, "is related to human development and passes through stages."[65] From the infant to the elderly person, "catechesis is thus a permanent school of the faith and follows the major stages of life."[66] The major stages of life that are recognized by the *NDC* are: adults, the elderly, young adults, adolescents, and infants and children. Also recognized are persons with disabilities and persons in special situations. Each stage/condition is treated in terms of the catechetical needs specific to each. However, overshadowed by the greater emphasis on the catechetical process(es) and evangelizing tone, the physical, social, and psychological conditions of each stage faintly are mentioned in the *NDC*. While catechists and parents are encouraged to receive appropriate training not only in scripture and theology but also in human development and catechetical methodology appropriate to each developmental stage,[67] the last two categories only are lightly touched upon throughout the Directory.

The *NDC*'s superficial treatment of the role of the social sciences in the catechetical process is a departure from its predecessor's (*Sharing the Light of Faith*) approach. The latter provides a deeper recognition of the behavioral sciences that is based on the statement: "These sciences do . . . help us understand how people grow in their capacity for responding to God's grace."[68]

The *National Directory for Catechesis* suggests, in the Catechesis of Adolescents section: "Catechesis for pre-adolescents and adolescents should take into account their physical, social, and psychological conditions."[69] Assuming that this pertains to all stages of human development, an in-depth education on the stages of human and faith development is needed for an enriching catechetical process to occur. However, the *NDC* does not offer scientific resources that would provide such education/information for those who catechize. Would it not be important that such resources be available? Which resources would facilitate such required knowledge? What theorists in the field of human and faith development provide scientific information that would be beneficial for the catechetical process?

The directory concurs with contemporary Catholic thought that adult catechesis is the principal form of catechesis for all persons in various stages of human and faith development. Does such consideration recognize that the goals, tasks, content, and methodologies of adult catechesis are similar for all the faithful including the elderly, children, adolescents, and young adults? In other words, is not the whole curriculum of the teaching ministry of the Church that is revealed under the category of adult catechesis, basically the curriculum for all Christian disciples who vary within the chronological and developmental dimensions of growing in faith? Assuming this is the case, then, does adult catechesis truly educate the adult learner or is adult catechesis only about initiation into the Church community and the transmission of the teachings of the Church? Is this true of all catechesis, at all levels of development? What is offered for the Christian who is considered to be mature in faith? What is offered for her/his continued education in the faith? Does the *NDC*'s meaning for *maturity in faith* allow room for questioning, criticizing, and resisting certain elements of one's tradition?

Finally, the Directory is concerned with Catholic maturity of faith. Can persons of other religious affiliations be considered mature in faith as well or is the term meant to be associated only with the Catholic Church? Does the field of religious education address the same issue? Does religious education offer an alternative vision of this regard?

THE MEANING OF "THE CONTEXT OF CATECHESIS" IN THE *NATIONAL DIRECTORY FOR CATECHESIS*

The context of catechesis is concerned with where the process of catechesis occurs. The movement toward universal schooling and making education available to all children have influenced a mindset of where catechesis takes place. Catechesis came to be specifically directed toward children and so formal catechetical instruction became associated with the classroom. Educational systems, synonymous with schooling for the most part, have fostered the idea that education is for children, with each grade level having its own set of tasks to be accomplished. The assumed completion of these tasks is celebrated with a graduation ceremony that can be seen by some to be a ritualistic symbol of termination of education on some level.

In light of these events, it is understandable to perceive an imbalance when greater emphasis has been placed on catechetical programs rather than on the catechetical process. Thomas Groome comments: "Like faith, education, in the richest sense of the term, is a whole and lifelong affair. Faith education, then includes schooling but requires much more; it demands the life of the faith community and all its forms."[70]

This section of the chapter will be concerned with how the *National Directory for Catechesis* treats the locus of where catechesis takes place as well as the persons who carry out the church's catechetical mission.

Where Catechesis Takes Place: The Context

While the *National Directory for Catechesis* establishes that catechesis is a lifelong process, it also establishes where the catechetical process should take place.

The directory acknowledges that the Church is the origin, locus, and goal of catechesis. It is the Church that provides the historical foundation, primary setting, and the goal for catechesis, which is to build up the Body of Christ on both the local and universal levels.[71] In carrying out this ecclesial action, the Church offers the natural environment for catechesis. The directory comments:

> [She] provides the primary setting for the proclamation of the Gospel, the point of welcome for those who seek to know the Lord, the place where men and women are invited to conversion and discipleship, the environment for the celebration of the sacraments, and the motivation for apostolic witness to the world.[72]

The Christian community is in and of itself a living catechesis.[73] It is the "context in which individuals undertake their journey in faith toward conversion to Christ and discipleship in his name.[74] Since the directory identifies 1) the parish and 2) the Christian family as the settings within the Christian community where catechesis takes place, it would be proper to determine the *NDC*'s description of these two catechetical loci.

1) The parish—for most people, the parish is the means for participation in the Christian community. It is the place where: a) the Christian faith is first received, expressed, and nourished; b) the Christian faith deepens and where the Christian community is formed; c) the members become aware of being the people of God; d) the faithful are nurtured by the Word of God and the sacraments, especially the Eucharist; and e) the faithful are sent on their apostolic mission in the world.[75] Also, according to the *NDC,* the parish 1) is a major point of reference for the Christian people, even the non-practicing; and 2) serves as an effective catechetical agent precisely to the extent that it is a clear, living, and authentic sacrament of Christ.[76]

However, if a parish appears lifeless and stagnant, it undermines both evangelization and catechesis. Therefore, "it is the responsibility of the parish community and its leadership to ensure that the faith that it teaches, preaches, and celebrates is alive and that it is a true sign for all who come in contact with it that this truly is the Body of Christ.[77]

2) The Christian Family—ordinarily the first experience of the Christian community is the Christian family. It is the primary environment for growth in faith. As the domestic church, the family provides a unique location for catechesis since it is a place where "the word of God is received and from which it is extended."[78]

The directory conforms with the conciliar document *Lumen Gentium* affirming that within the Christian family the parents are the primary educators in the faith. They are "the first heralds of the faith with regard to their children."[79] The directory also contends that all family members can make a unique contribution to creating an environment where the sense of God's presence can be awakened and where faith in Jesus Christ may be acknowledged, encouraged, and lived.[80]

The *NDC* upholds that the Christian community is the locus of catechesis and that the effectiveness of catechesis depends on the vitality of the Christian community in which catechesis takes place. However, such a notion presents some questions. First, what is meant by the term *effective catechesis?* How, if possible, can such effectiveness be measured? Second, what are the criteria that mark a vital faith community? Even though the *NDC* presents forms that would add to a parish's vitality, such as nourishing Christian faith through the Eucharist and the Word of God, forming Christian community, and keeping the doors always open, are these forms in and of themselves enough to produce a vital parish community?

Likewise, what determines a Christian family as seen through the eyes of the Catholic Church? Is the family more than a herald of the faith? What are the specific dynamics for parents in their passing on the Catholic tradition while living in the contemporary world? What if all family members are not Christian or Catholic? Is there room for the Catholic family that does not appear to fit the familial ideal as proposed by the Church? Answers to such questions appear to be absent from the *National Directory for Catechesis.* However, the signs of the times call for such queries to be discussed.

Perhaps in order for educational ministry to be effective and life-giving, the catechist and the parish as a whole must be aware of the curriculum of the Church as well as the fundamental forms of the Church's life. To understand this concept more in depth, one can look to the work of Maria Harris. This will be done in the subsequent chapters.

Catechists: Those Who Carry Out the Church's Catechetical Mission

In Chapter 8, the *National Directory for Catechesis* clearly states: " . . . all members of the community of believers in Jesus Christ participate in the Church's catechetical mission."[81] However, some members are called to a specific role within this mission. Those who have distinctive roles would be parents, parish catechists and catechetical leaders for adults and children, Catholic school principals and teachers, youth ministry leaders, those who work in diocesan and national catechetical offices, deacons, consecrated religious, priests, and bishops.[82] The *NDC* provides the particulars of these distinctive roles.

Although all members of the faith community share in the responsibility of the Catholic Church's catechetical mission, it is the bishop who has primary responsibility for the total catechetical mission of the local church. He is the "chief catechist" who is to carry out the fundamental task of catechesis. As a catechist himself, the bishop is a "herald of faith," who, through the power of the Holy Spirit, has been constituted a true and authentic teacher. The *NDC* explains:

> This derives from the individual bishop's relationship with the whole Church, whose faith he articulates. In his diocese, the bishop "has a unique and authoritative role in teaching the faith of the Catholic Church in the particular church that is given to his care." In his own preaching and teaching, the bishop transmits the teachings of Christ—the teachings of the entire Church. By his profound conviction of the importance of catechesis for the Christian life of his diocese, the bishop should bring about and maintain "a real passion for catechesis.[83]

However, the *NDC* makes it clear that bishops are not to work alone. They are to share the responsibility of carrying out the church's catechetical mission with highly skilled and professional diocesan catechetical personnel as well as competent teachers and catechists who proclaim the "authentic Gospel of Jesus Christ and hand on the complete and accurate deposit of faith."[84]

As the bishop's closest collaborators in ensuring the achievement of the diocese's catechetical mission, pastors have specific catechetical roles. Basically, pastors are responsible for catechesis and for proper sacramental preparation, celebration, and reception for all members of the parish. Working with parents, school and catechetical personnel, and appropriate parish boards and commissions, the pastor has "the primary responsibility to ensure that the catechetical needs, goals, and priorities of the parish are identified, articulated, and met."[85]

Priests, who are the immediate collaborators with the bishops in proclaiming the Gospel, share in the teaching role of their bishops. This particular role they exercise "arises directly from the Sacrament of Holy Orders, which constitutes priests as educators in the faith."[86] The priest is called to be the *catechist of catechists,* who 1) transmits the Gospel; 2) encourages conversion to Jesus Christ; 3) fosters the life of faith and ongoing formation in faith; 5) inspires the prayer of the faith community; 6) offers support to all those involved in catechesis; 7) plays an active role in collaborating with catechetical leaders to provide catechists with formation and support; and 8) plays an active role in the catechetical programs and is available to celebrate the sacraments with classes and groups. Importantly, priests are "to give careful attention to their own catechetical formation and continue their education and spiritual formation after ordination."[87]

Likewise, as candidates for the priesthood, seminarians are to have a clear understanding of the nature, goals, and methods of catechesis. Therefore, seminarians should learn the processes of human growth and development and faith formation, so that they will be able to adapt the Gospel message to the age and ability of those they catechize, as well as an understanding of and training in the organization and supervision of the catechetical ministry in the parish. This would include sensitivity to the diversity of cultures that are part of the Catholic Church in the United States.[88]

Deacons are to serve the faith community in the ministry of the Word in communion with the bishop and the priests. As participants in the catechetical ministry, deacons should receive formation that includes study in theology, liturgy, Sacred Scripture, catechesis, and communication skills. If a deacon is to serve as a parish or diocesan leader, he should receive proper catechetical training.[89]

Women and men in consecrated life witness to their commitment to the mission of the church. They have and continue to have an impact on the catechetical ministry in the United States. However, women and men in consecrated life are to receive appropriate training if they are to serve as parish or diocesan leaders.[90]

Since the leadership of a professionally trained parish catechetical leader is the most critical factor in an effective parish catechetical program, parishes should allocate their resources in order to acquire the services of a competent and qualified catechetical leader.[91] Under the direction of the pastor, the parish catechetical leader 1) is responsible for the overall catechetical programs for adults, youth, and children; 2) plans, implements, and evaluates the parish catechetical program; 3) is responsible for the recruitment, formation, ongoing development, and evaluation of catechists; 4) implements diocesan and parish policies and guidelines; 5) collaborates with the pastor, other parish ministers, and appropriate committees and councils; 6) assists in liturgical planning; and 7) attends to her/his own personal, spiritual, and professional development. In addition, parish catechetical leaders are full members of the parish pastoral staff.[92]

Youth ministers are those who should be capable to lead and guide young people to grow in the knowledge of the Catholic faith, in the practice of that faith in light of the principles of Christian morality and social justice, in sacramental celebrations, and in the development of their spiritual lives. Coordinators of youth ministry should always be in collaboration with the pastor and the parish catechetical leader.[93]

Campus ministers provide the proclamation of the Gospel within the academic community in order to "build up the Church on campus."[94] Campus ministry should initiate courses of study that provide theological education, spiritual formation, and practical experience to strengthen students' knowledge of faith as well as to prepare them to serve in the catechetical ministry. In addition, campus ministers should work for "responsible governance and evaluate the institution's programs, policies, and research in the light of Catholic social doctrine."[95]

The *NDC* acknowledges that catechists are called to the catechetical ministry through "the voice of the Holy Spirit."[96] A vocation to this apostolic work is generated from the sacrament of baptism "through which all believers come to share in the prophetic ministry of Christ and the evangelizing mission of the Church."[97]

The catechist, like all the faithful, is called to holiness, and so the spiritual life of the catechist has a particular urgency that is to be nourished and characterized by the active practice of the Catholic faith. Catechists are to minister by 1) proclaiming the Gospel; 2) sharing their personal testimony; and 3) witnessing, through their own lives, the transcendent values of Christian life. They are to be attentive to adapt their catechetical methodology to the needs of particular groups as well as create an environment where the Christian message is sought, accepted, and profoundly investigated. Therefore, catechists are to be prepared for their apostolate by appropriate catechetical training and ongoing formation that is to be provided and developed by parishes and dioceses.[98]

Catholic schools are considered to be effective vehicles of total Christian formation. Like parish catechetical programs, the catechetical instruction of the Catholic school should be based on the *Catechism of the Catholic Church,* and such programs should be coordinated with the catechetical plan of the parish(es) to which they are connected.[99]

The Catholic school principal, under the direction of the pastor or school board, has the responsibility of being the catechetical leader, ensuring that the school's catechetical program is essential to Catholic identity and character. This is to be accomplished by 1) recognizing that all members of the faculty and staff are an integral part of the process of religious education; 2) recruiting new teachers who are practicing Catholics, who can understand and accept the teachings of the Catholic Church and the moral demands of the Gospel; 3) supervising, through evaluation and observation, the performance of each religion teacher; 4) providing opportunities for ongoing catechesis for faculty members; 5) designing a curriculum that supports the school's catechetical goals; 6) implementing an overall catechetical plan for the school and evaluating its progress; 7) fostering a distinctively Christian community among the faculty, students, and parents; 8) providing, along with the pastor, for the spiritual growth of the faculty; and 9) collaborating with parish, area, and diocesan personnel in planning and implementing programs of total parish catechesis.[100]

The *NDC* states: "Religion teachers in Catholic schools not only teach the Catholic faith as an academic subject but also bear witness to the truth of what they teach."[101] In other words, religion teachers have the same responsibilities and perform many of the same functions as parish catechists. Actually, all Catholic schoolteachers share in the catechetical ministry. Therefore, they also must meet the diocesan standards for certification as a catechist.[102]

Parents are not only the first educators of their children; they also are catechists, since "they catechize primarily by the witness of their Christian lives and by their love for the faith."[103] The primary catechesis that occurs within the family accompanies and enriches all other forms of catechesis. Therefore, programs designed for the faith education of parents are necessary in order to meet the catechetical and spiritual needs of the Christian family.[104]

It appears that, while catechetical roles presented in the *National Directory for Catechesis* are distinct, their common bond is that persons who embrace these roles are catechists in their own right. In other words, if the whole faith community is responsible for the carrying out the catechetical mission of the Church, it would seem reasonable, then, that all who catechize should possess certain qualities that are promulgated in the *NDC*. Therefore, it is apparent that whatever role one is called to within the Church's catechetical mission, there are particular stipulations for all catechists regardless of role distinction.

The Church delegates the catechetical ministry to "exemplary followers of Christ with unquestioned personal integrity and moral character."[105] The Directory duplicates the thought within the Vatican document *Guide for Catechists* (1993), presented by the Congregation for the Evangelization of Peoples:

> Positive qualities in candidates should be: faith that manifests itself in their piety and daily life; love for the Church and communion with its pastors; apostolic spirit and missionary zeal; love for their brothers and sisters and a willingness to give generous service; sufficient education; the respect of the community; the human, moral and technical qualities necessary for the work of a catechist; such as dynamism, good relations with others, etc.[106]

The Directory continues:

> Like all Christians, catechists are called to continual conversion and growth in their faith and, for this reason, are called to ongoing spiritual formation through

frequent reception of the sacraments, especially the Sacraments of the Holy Eucharist and Reconciliation, through spiritual direction, and through continued study of the faith. The catechist should also be provided with opportunities for spiritual growth such as retreats, conferences, etc. In addition to spiritual formation, the catechist is also in need of pedagogical formation, especially as society, teaching methods, and culture change.[107]

The Directory stipulates that all catechists need to be properly trained and formed in order to carry out the evangelical and catechetical aspirations of the Catholic Church. However, in doing so, the Directory positions itself for questioning.

Since bishops, the *chief catechists* of dioceses,[108] are constituted as true teachers by the power of the Holy Spirit, and priests are constituted as educators through the sacrament of Holy Orders,[109] does that mean they are so without proper training in teaching and educational methodologies? Is this a possible misuse of the terms *to teach* and *to educate?*

Interestingly, those who are called to catechize in parish programs are called to ministry. However, those who are called to teach religion in Catholic schools are called to *religious education,* to teach religion as an academic subject. Yet, the *NDC* names such teachers as *catechists* as well. Is the teacher of religion a catechist? Another distinction also arises here. Catholic-school religion teachers are salaried, while catechists in parish programs for the most part are volunteers. Yet each is required to receive proper training and formation. Does that mean that those who *minister* in a parish are to do so without benefit of salary while others who teach in a different setting are salaried? If religion can be taught as an academic subject in Catholic schools, can such an endeavor also be achieved in a parish setting? Where can children and youth/young adults, who do not attend a Catholic school, and Catholic adults be religiously educated? Since the family also is a setting for catechesis, how will and who will implement and encourage appropriate formation for parents and will parents be empowered to catechize their children?

The Directory calls for a collaboration between dioceses and Catholic colleges and universities in order to provide formal education for those who embrace the educational mission of the Catholic Church. Catholic institutes of higher learning can offer "the totality of the Christian message, a thorough knowledge of the sociocultural situation, and sound catechetical methodology to all catechists from all parts of the diocese."[110] Can such collaboration offer solutions that might enrich the catechetical mission of the church? Is there an inherent tension between academic processes and parish catechetical processes? Is the *who* of catechesis the same as the *who* of religious education?

METHODOLOGIES IN CATECHETICAL EDUCATION
IN THE *NATIONAL DIRECTORY FOR CATECHESIS*

The *National Directory for Catechesis* offers two fundamental methods for conveying the Gospel message. These methods, *divine methodology* and *human methodology*, working together, are the means of communication of faith in catechesis. In addition, *liturgical catechesis* needs to be recognized as a component of catechetical methodology since it provides a specific form of methodology. We now will address the meanings of these methods established in the *NDC*. We begin with *divine methodology*.

Divine Methodology

The *National Directory for Catechesis* postulates that the purpose of God's divine plan is for the salvation of humankind. *Divine methodology* is the way God reveals the mystery of God's divine plan through the loving communion of the Father, Son, and Holy Spirit. The *NDC* explicates:

> God's own methodology engages persons and communities in light of their circumstances and their capacity to accept and interpret Revelation. God's self-communication is realized gradually through his actions and his words. It is most fully achieved in the Word made flesh, Jesus Christ. The history of this self-revelation itself documents the method by which God transmits the content of Revelation as contained in Sacred Scripture and Tradition. This is the pedagogy of God. It is the source and model of the pedagogy of faith.[111]

The pedagogy of God reflects the work of revelation that is the common work and actions of the three divine persons within the Trinity. As repeated in the *NDC,* the Father is revealed in creation, through the covenant experiences of the people of Israel, and in the eternal Word, Jesus Christ. The redemptive mission of the Son, Jesus Christ, continues the pedagogy of God in the history of salvation. As the preeminent model for the communication of the faith and the formation of believers in the faith, Jesus, through the mystery of his incarnation, joins divinity with humanity in teaching the faith and forming disciples. Jesus' methodology serves as a model for all catechetical methods. His words, signs, compassion for marginalized persons, his proclamation of the Kingdom of God, the forgiveness of sins and reconciliation with the Father, his use of parables, his prayer, his death and resurrection, reveal the many dimensions of his methodology. The Holy Spirit continues the pedagogy of God in the Church, unfolding the divine plan of salvation within the Church. Constantly seeking to discover the most fruitful way to announce the Good News, the Church first looks to the method used by God. The Church, then, continues God's own methodology in a living catechesis.[112]

Catechesis and Divine Methodology

As a communication of divine revelation, catechesis is inspired by the pedagogy of God as displayed in Jesus Christ and the Church. In light of this principle, catechesis 1) conveys God's loving plan of salvation in the person of Jesus Christ; 2) emphasizes God's initiative in this plan, his attentive disclosure of it, and his respect for individual liberty; 3) recognizes the dignity of the human person within this profound dialogue with God and the continual need for conversion; 4) acknowledges the gradual nature of God's self-revelation, the profound mystery of the growth of God's word in a person, and the need for adaptation to different persons and cultures; 5) keeps Jesus Christ at its center in order to bring humanity to God and God to humanity; and 6) constantly draws inspiration from the Holy Spirit, who unfolds the mystery of Jesus in the Church.[113]

The methods that catechesis engages harmonize the personal faithfulness of the believer to God with the content of the Christian message. It does so by: 1) attending to the development of all the dimensions of the faith as it is known, as it is celebrated, as it is lived, and as it is prayed; 2) seeking to bring about a conversion to Jesus Christ that leads to a profession of faith in the Triune God and to a genuine surrender to [him]; 3) helping believers to become disciples; and 4) facilitating in the disciple's vocational discernment.[114]

Contemporary catechesis is to use a plurality of methods that must exhibit 1) faithfulness to God and to his Revelation; and 2) a respect for the liberty and active participation of those being catechized. Concerning methodology, the *NDC* recommends that catechesis should employ the following: 1) an emphasis on God's loving initiative and the person's free response; 2) an acceptance of the progressive nature of Revelation, the transcendence and mysterious nature of the word of God, and the word's adaptation to different persons and cultures; 3) a recognition of the centrality of Jesus Christ; 4) an appreciation of the community experience of faith; 5) a grounding in interpersonal relationships and in making its own process of dialogue; 6) the use of signs that link words and deeds, teaching and experience; and 7) drawing the power of truth from the Holy Spirit in order to bear witness to the truth from the Holy Spirit.[115]

Attentive to and through the employment of *divine methodology*, catechesis should deepen the believer's understanding of the mystery of Jesus Christ thus leading the believer to conversion and to a life of discipleship. It also should develop a blending of the faith that has been taught to believe with the faith that is enacted in daily life. Catechesis is to develop all dimensions of faith that is: knowledge, liturgical celebration, Christian living, and prayer. In other words, it implements "the complete work of initiation, education and teaching."[116]

Catechesis uses God's own methodology as the paradigm and divine pedagogy as the reference point in the process of transmitting the faith. However, a diversity of human methodologies that harmonize content and method is needed "to ensure that the Gospel is proclaimed to all the nations."[117]

Elements of Human Methodology

The *National Directory for Catechesis* acknowledges that the communication of faith through catechesis is "an event of grace under the action of the Holy Spirit, realized in the encounter of the Word of God with the experience of the person . . . (through this process) an individual hears the Word of God through catechesis and is moved by the Holy Spirit to listen, consider, assent to the truth, and respond through the obedience of faith."[118]

There are two basic processes engaged by catechetical methods that organize the human element in the communication of faith. These are the *inductive method* and the *deductive method*. The former consists of presenting facts such as biblical events, liturgical acts, events in the life of the church, and events from daily life, discerning the meaning they might have in connection with divine Revelation; the latter begins with the general principles or truths of the faith as expressed in Sacred Scripture, the creeds, and the liturgy and applies them to particular human experience. According to the *NDC,* "Both are legitimate approaches when properly applied and are distinct yet complementary methods for communicating the faith."[119]

The Directory offers eight elements to catechetical methodology. These elements are:

a) Learning through human experience—Catechesis connects human experience to the revealed word of God, helping persons to explore, interpret, and judge their basic experiences in light of the Gospel.
b) Learning by discipleship—catechesis nourishes the living, explicit, and fruitful faith that is lived in discipleship to Jesus Christ, marked by intimate communion with him.
c) Learning within the Christian community—the Christian community provides the context for catechesis where individuals journey in their faith. As a catechetical agent, the parish serves as an effective catechetical agent

precisely to the extent that it is a clear, living, and authentic sacrament of
Christ ensuring that the faith it teaches, preaches, and celebrates is a sign
that it is the living Body of Christ.

d) Learning within the Christian family—the family offers informal rather
than systematic catechetical instruction. The Christian family provides the
basic environment where a sense of God's loving presence is first stimulated and faith in Jesus Christ is professed and lived. This is manifested
through the learning of the basic teachings of Jesus Christ and the church
that includes conscience formation in the light of the Gospel.

e) Learning through the witness of the catechist—catechists are influential
by their faithful proclamation of the Gospel of Jesus Christ and through
the transparent example of their Christian lives. The role of the catechist
is to hand on the teachings of Christ. This is accomplished through: 1)
sacramental preparation; 2) orientation toward a life lived according to the
moral teaching of Christ; and 3) direction in prayer with Christ.

f) Learning by heart—acknowledging that the living tradition of the faith has
been handed on principally through oral tradition, the *NDC* emphasizes
that effective catechesis is to incorporate *learning by heart.* The Directory also implies that such a methodology should be incorporated into
contemporary catechesis in order that the principal formulations of the
faith (basic prayers, key biblical themes, personalities, expressions, and
factual information regarding worship and Christian life) might provide
an accurate exposition of the faith. This methodology provides the ability
to express the one faith in a language of the faith among all the faithful.
It allows for the reception of the formulations of the faith, the professing
and internalizing of these formulations, and, in turn, sharing them with the
community. Such a process should encourage the individual's participation in the *received truth.* In addition, the memorization of psalms, songs,
prayers, and poetry in praise of Christ nourishes the human heart, forming
the human spirit in Christ.

g) Making a commitment to live the Christian life—an essential catechetical
methodology is learning by Christian living. Fostering learning by doing
is a crucial element in effective catechetical methodology. Such methodology encompasses the active participation of all the catechized through:
1) praying; 2) celebrating the sacraments and the liturgy; 3) living the
Christian life; 4) fostering works of charity (meeting the immediate needs
of the poor and vulnerable); 5) works of justice (working to address the
injustices that exist in the systemic and institutional organizations of society); 6) the promotion of virtues from the natural law such as liberty,
solidarity, justice, peace, and the protection of the created order; and 7) the
participation of adults in their own catechetical formation.

h) Learning by apprenticeship—this type of catechetical methodology unites an experienced Christian believer with one who seeks a deeper relationship with Christ and the church. In addition to catechetical instruction, this methodology fosters a guided encounter with the entire Christian life and a journey towards conversion to Christ. It is a school for discipleship, where one accepts one's own baptismal responsibilities, the internalization of the Word of God, and the transformation of the whole person to a life in Christ.[120]

Liturgical Catechesis

The Catholic/Christian faith community, then, provides the *where* and *who* of catechesis. However, it should be acknowledged that as the faith community gathers to worship, it is the act of worship that renews the faith of the community. In the liturgy, the official worship of the church, the community celebrates what it professes and lives. Through the rituals and rites of the church, the faithful can relate their experiences with the Paschal Mystery that is the soteriological work of Jesus Christ.[121]

Liturgy and catechesis are related in that they both share in the church's mission of evangelization. Both proclaim the Gospel, initiate believers into the Christian life, and look for the coming of the fullness of the kingdom. Liturgy is the privileged place for catechizing the People of God. The *NDC* notes: "The history of salvation, from the creation of the world to its redemption and eschatological fulfillment in Jesus Christ, is celebrated in the sacraments, especially the Eucharist."[122]

Liturgical catechesis is pedagogical in that it prepares the faithful for active participation in the church's liturgical celebrations and it imparts an identity that is Roman Catholic. The *NDC* elaborates on this notion:

Catechesis both precedes the Liturgy and springs from it. It prepares people for a full, conscious, and active participation in the Liturgy by helping them understand its nature, rites, and symbols. It stems from the Liturgy insofar as it helps people to worship God and to reflect on their experience of the words, signs, rituals, and symbols expressed in the Liturgy; to discern the implications of their participation in the Liturgy; and to respond to its missionary summons to bear witness and offer service. And liturgy itself is inherently catechetical. As the Scriptures are proclaimed and reflected upon and as the Creed is articulated, the truths of the faith shape more and more profoundly the faith of the People of God. Through the Eucharist, the People of God come to know the Paschal Mystery ever more intimately and experientially. They come not simply to the knowledge of God—they come to know the living God.[123]

Within the context of liturgical catechesis and in conformity with various preceding catechetical documents and directories, the *National Directory for Catechesis* stresses that the baptismal catechumenate "is the source of inspiration for all catechesis."[124] This formative process is both catechetical and liturgical in that it: 1) instructs the catechumen through a progression of gradual stages, unfolding the Church's rites, symbols, and biblical and liturgical signs; and 2) it incorporates the catechumen into the Christian community of faith and worship, in particular through the sacraments of initiation: Baptism, Confirmation and Eucharist.[125]

The four stages of the baptismal catechumenate include: 1) the *pre-catechumenate* that coincides with the first evangelization; 2) the *catechumenate* that is accompanied by the handing on of the Gospels to the catechumen and/or candidate and presenting a more integral and systematic catechesis; 3) *purification and enlightenment* that is characterized by the celebration of the scrutinies, more intense prayer, and study and conferral of the Creed and the Lord's Prayer; and 4) *mystogogy* that is the post-baptismal catechesis that marks the time in which the neophyte experiences the sacraments and fully enters into the life of the community. *The Rite of Initiation of Adults* (1988) sets forth the directives that follow throughout the process of initiation of adults and children of catechetical age into the life of the Church. [126] In a word, historically, and in contemporary catechetical texts, the link between liturgy and catechesis has been close and is reinforced in the *National Directory for Catechesis*.

The *NDC* concludes that catechetical methodology will always be the work of the Trinity. Although catechists employ a variety of methodologies, the Triune God is the paradigm for catechetical methodology in transmitting knowledge of the faith. In other words, God's own methodology "always remains the model for all human methodologies."[127] But is catechesis the only form of faith education that uses the Trinity as its methodological model? Does the field of religious education depend upon a *divine methodology* or are these exclusively Catholic processes? If this be the case, is the revelation of God exclusive to Catholics? How is God revealed to those who do not have a Trinitarian theology as a tenet of faith? Are inductive and deductive methods and *learning by heart* sufficient in and of themselves or are there additional educational methodologies that could enrich the catechetical process? The *National Directory for Catechesis* emphasizes the learning component in the eight elements of human methodology. What about the teaching component? Are not both teaching and learning part of the educative process? While catechists and their role(s) are considered in the directory, can they truly be considered *teachers* in the fullest meaning of the term? Are catechists trained to be only transmitters of the faith or are they expected to be more? Is there a place for critical dialogue and dialectical discussion? Are catechists teachers of religion or should they be? These queries will be addressed in the following chapters.

THE THEOLOGICAL FOUNDATIONS OF CATECHESIS IN THE *NATIONAL DIRECTORY FOR CATECHESIS*

In the contemporary United States, catechesis is to be implemented by five distinct yet complementary instruments. These are: Sacred Scripture, the *Catechism of the Catholic Church* (1997), the *General Directory for Catechesis* (1997), the new *National Directory for Catechesis* (2005) and the pastoral *Our Hearts Were Burning Within Us* (1999). The *GDC* provides basic principles of pastoral theology; the *NDC* includes general guidelines for catechesis in the U.S.; and *OHWB* provides a plan and strategies for effective adult faith formation. However, Sacred Scripture, the cornerstone of catechesis,[128] and the *Catechism of the Catholic Church,* the doctrinal point of reference for catechesis,[129] provide the theological bases for the Christian message that is to be echoed through the catechetical ministry. It should be noted, however, that by its design, the *Catechism of the Catholic Church,* does not provide an adaptation of doctrinal presentations and catechetical methodologies. It would be the responsibility of particular catechisms and those who instruct the faithful to carry out such a task.[130]

The theological foundations of the Catholic faith, stated in the *Catechism of the Catholic Church* are the "what" or the content for the catechetical ministry. These foundations are based upon the initial creedal statements of the early Christian church. These statements have been the substance of the Christian message.

In this section, four theological foundations/categories, denoted in the *National Directory for Catechesis* in the section titled, *Criteria for the Authentic Presentation of the Christian Message,* will be presented. These foundations/categories are: 1) The Christian Message, Centered on Christ; 2) The Trinitarian Character of the Christian Message; 3) The Ecclesial Character of the Christian Message; and 4) The Profound Meaning of the Human Person: Christian Anthropology. We now turn to the directory's treatment of these theological foundations, as well as to the questions they might incite.

The Christian Message, Centered on Jesus Christ

Since the Christian message focuses on the person of Jesus the Christ, all catechesis must transmit the centrality of Jesus in the Gospel message.

Centering on Jesus and his Paschal Mystery, the document presents Jesus
as the center of salvation history. The *NDC* explains: "As the definitive
Revelation of God, he is the point in salvation history toward which the
created order proceeds from the beginning of time and the final event toward which it converges . . . He is 'the key, the center and the purpose of
the whole of [man's] history.'"[131]

Jesus' proclamation of the good news of the kingdom of God marks a new
and definitive intervention by God. Tantamount to Jesus' good news is salvation and liberation for all. Liberation, in this sense, refers to the fundamental
form of freedom, that is, the liberation from sin. Such a message frees the
oppressed so they might be open to the working of the Holy Spirit in their
lives.[132]

It would appear, that the theology of Christocentricity, in the manner of
which it is presented in the *National Directory for Catechesis,* is focused on
the divinity of Jesus Christ, thus underplaying the human, historical Jesus.
Might such a focus be an obstacle in dialogue with other religions? Are its
claims exclusive and monopolistic?

The Trinitarian Character of the Christian Message

The mystery of the Triune God is central to the Catholic faith. It is a profession of faith whose fundamental doctrinal formulations state Christian
belief in the Father, the Son, and the Holy Spirit.[133] The doctrine of the
Trinity confesses that God is Father, Son, and Holy Spirit; one God in three
divine persons. Who God is and what God does form a unity of divine life
and activity. In other words, the inner life of the Trinity and the actions
of the divine persons are undivided and inseparable. While the work of
revelation is the common work of the three divine persons, each person
of the Trinity shows forth what is proper to each within the one divine
nature.[134]

The Christian message and the Christian life are essentially Trinitarian
since their source Jesus Christ, the incarnate Word of the Father who speaks
to the world through his Holy Spirit. Therefore, the primary subject of catechesis is the mystery of the Holy Trinity that makes available vital implications for Christian living.[135]

Is the Trinitarian theology, as realized in the *NDC,* rooted in Augustinian
thought that focuses on the inner life, *in se* of the Trinity? On the other hand,
Cappadocian theology stresses a *pro nobis* doctrine professing that Father,
Son, and Holy Spirit are operational in the economy of salvation. Can the
doctrine of the Trinity, as it is presented in the Directory, be linked with the
daily demands of Christian life? Or is it ahistorical and detached from current
events?[136]

The Ecclesial Character of the Christian Message

Beginning with Jesus' mandate to the apostles to announce the coming of God's kingdom of love, justice, and peace, the message has resounded through the ages. While the kingdom already was present in Jesus and the church, it was not yet fulfilled. The *NDC* affirms: "The mission of Christ and the Holy Spirit is brought to completion in the Church, which is the Body of Christ and the Temple of the Holy Spirit . . . This divine mission that Jesus entrusted to his Church will continue until the end of time."[137] Jesus pledged to be with his Church until the end of time and this promise is the source of great hope for the whole Church since all members share in its mission through various ways. However, all members must recognize that the fruitfulness of the mission depends exclusively on their vital union with Jesus Christ.[138]

The Christian community, bound together by the gospel message, continues to convey the gospel message throughout the world. Catechesis comes forth from the Church's confession of faith and then, in turn, leads the community to the profession of faith. The ecclesial character of catechesis encourages it to: 1) transmit the one faith to all peoples; 2) introduce catechumens and those to be catechized to the unity of the profession of faith; and 3) nourish the Body of Christ.[139] In a word, catechesis is the work of the ecclesia, by the ecclesia, for the ecclesia, for the sake of the world.

However, is the work of the Church, as described in the *NDC,* compatible with the work of other church bodies or does it represent a form of religious imperialism? Is this ecclesiology capable of engaging in discourse, conversing in contemporary issues, in the public square?

The Profound Meaning of the Human Person: Christian Anthropology

According to the *NDC,* the human person is a mystery.[140] Human beings are created in the image and likeness of God. The divine image is present in every person. Redemption in Christ intensifies the inherent dignity of the person.[141]

Through Jesus, persons learn how to live their lives; yet God created persons with the freedom to initiate and direct their own actions and to shape their own lives. The *NDC* states: "Every human person is a free and responsible agent with an unalienable right to exercise freedom, especially in moral and religious matters."[142] However, with human freedom comes the capacity to choose good or evil. Choosing to do what is good brings about more freedom for the human person, while choosing what is evil is an abuse of freedom and "leads to the 'slavery of sin.'"[143]

Various situations can challenge the dignity of the human person. Some of these situations might contradict the Christian understanding of human dignity and freedom. Therefore, there is a need for a moral catechesis that "involves more than the proclamation and presentation of the principles and practice of Christian morality. It presents the integration of moral principles in the lived experience of the individual and the community. This moral testimony must always demonstrate the social consequences of the Gospel."[144] The content for moral catechesis is to include the ideologies of grace, virtue, sin, and the formation of moral conscience.

The human person lives within the tension of good and evil. Which side does the *NDC* stress? Is it a Catholic anthropology that stresses the dignity, sacramentality and sacredness of the human person? Or is it more compatible with a Protestant anthropology of fallenness and sin?

SUMMARY

Through a theoretical analysis of the *National Directory for Catechesis* conducted in this chapter, we have revealed the contemporary meaning of catechesis and catechetics, especially as it is addressed in the Roman Catholic Church of the United States.

Such an endeavor has been achieved through the analysis of the major themes that are presented throughout the directory. An examination of these themes: 1) the meaning and identity of catechesis; 2) the meaning of "maturity in faith"; 3) the context of catechesis; 4) methodology in catechetical education; and 5) the theological foundations of the document, have unveiled the "what," "where," "who," "when," "how," and "why" of contemporary catechesis.

A spirit of critique has exposed some of the strengths and weaknesses of the document without marring the document's proclaimed purpose, vision, place within the history of catechetical renewal, and its role in the development of catechesis in the United States. However, we should keep in mind, the multiple questions posed throughout this chapter. We are reminded of the following examples: Does positioning the meaning of catechesis only within the context of evangelization prevent catechesis from growing and developing into something more than it is or can be? Does the *NDC*'s meaning for *maturity in faith* allow room for questioning, critiquing, and resisting certain elements of one's tradition? What are the criteria that mark a vital faith community? Is the teacher of religion a catechist as well? Are catechists trained to be only transmitters of the faith or are they expected to be more? Are *inductive* and *deductive methods* and *learning by heart* sufficient in and of themselves or are there additional educational methodologies that could enrich the catechetical process? Are the theological foundations presented in the *NDC* so absolute that they cannot withstand engaging in discourse? Could catechesis benefit from engagement with a missing partner in the *NDC*, namely, religious education?

The first partner in this work, the *National Directory for Catechesis* has been unveiled. The next chapter will address the second partner, *religious education,* where we will explore its meaning, contemporary thought, and its contributions to the process of educating religiously. In doing so, the "what," "where," "who," "when," "how," and "why" of contemporary religious education will be undertaken in the same manner as the first partner.

NOTES

1. Committee on Education and Committee on Catechesis, *National Directory for Catechesis* (Washington D.C.: United States Conference of Catholic Bishops, 2005) no. 5.

2. Congregation for the Clergy. *General Directory for Catechesis* (Libreria Editrice Vaticana, 1997) no. 35.

3. *The New Oxford American Dictionary,* ed. Elizabeth J. Jewell and Frank Abate (Oxford: Oxford University Press, 2001).

4. The meaning of *catechesis* in this study is that of the *National Directory for Catechesis.* It could be argued that there are alternative meanings of *catechesis* in ecclesial documents such as in *Sharing the Light of Faith.* But the working meaning throughout this book is from the *National Directory for Catechesis.*

5. The Gospel According to Mark 16:15 in t*he New American Catholic Bible, Personal Study Edition.* New York: Oxford University Press, 1995.

6. The Gospel According to Mark 16:20.

7. *National Directory for Catechesis* no.15.

8. Pope Paul VI, "Evangelii Nuntiandi" no.14, in *The Catechetical Documents: A Parish Resource* 161 (Chicago: Liturgy Training Publications, 1996).

9. See John Paul II, *Redemptoris Missio,* no. 3.

10. Thomas Groome, "Total Catechesis/Religious Education: A Vision for Now and Always" *Horizons and Hopes: The Future of Religious Education,* ed. Thomas H Groome and Harold Daly Horell, 2 (Mahwah: Paulist Press, 2003).

11. *National Directory for Catechesis,* no.15.

12. Thomas P. Walters, "Overview of *On Evangelization in the Modern World"* in *The Catechetical Documents: A Parish Resource,* 150 (Chicago: Liturgy Training Publications, 1996).

13. Catherine Dooley, "Evangelization and Catechesis: Partners in the New Millenium" in *The Echo Within: Emerging Issues in Religious Education,* ed. Catherine Dooley and Mary Collins, 153 (Allen, TX: Thomas More, 1997).

14. Pope John Paul II, "On Catechesis in Our Time" no. 18 in *The Catechetical Documents: A Parish Resource,* 383 (Chicago: Liturgy Training Publications, 1996).

15. Pope John Paul II, *Redemptoris Missio* cited in Catherine Dooley, O.P. "Evangelization and Catechesis: Partners in the New Millenium", 154.

16. *The New Oxford American Dictionary,* ed. Elizabeth J. Jewell and Frank Abate, (Oxford: Oxford University Press, 2001).

17. *Go and Make Disciples: A National Plan and Strategy for Catholic Evangelization in the United States* (Washington, D.C.: National Conference of Catholic Bishops, November 18, 1992), 4.

18. *National Directory for Catechesis*, no.17, sect. A.

19. *National Directory for Catechesis,* no.17, sect. C.

20. *National Directory for Catechesis,* no.17, sect. C.

21. *National Directory for Catechesis,* no.17, sect. E.

22. The title of Chapter Two of the *National Directory for Catechesis* is "Catechesis Within the Church's Mission of Evangelization."

23. *National Directory for Catechesis,* no. 15.

24. *National Directory for Catechesis,* no. 17, sect. E.

25. *National Directory for Catechesis,* no. 17, sect. E.

26. *National Directory for Catechesis,* no. 17, sect. C.

27. *National Directory for Catechesis,* no. 19, sect. A.

28. *National Directory for Catechesis,* no. 22.

29. *National Directory for Catechesis,* no. 17, sect. C.

30. *National Directory for Catechesis,* no. 19, sect. A.

31. *National Directory for Catechesis,* no. 19, sect. A.

32. *National Directory for Catechesis,* no. 19, sect. C.

33. *National Directory for Catechesis,* no. 20.

34. *National Directory for Catechesis,* no. 20.

35. *National Directory for Catechesis,* no. 20.

36. *National Directory for Catechesis,* no. 20.

37. *National Directory for Catechesis,* no. 20.

38. *National Directory for Catechesis,* no. 20.

39. *National Directory for Catechesis,* no. 22.

40. Dooley, "Evangelization and Catechesis: Partners in the New Millennium," 154.

41. Dooley, "Evangelization and Catechesis: Partners in the New Millenium," 155.

42. The Letter of Paul to the Ephesians (4:11–13) in *The New American Catholic Bible, Personal Study Edition* (New York: Oxford University Press, 1995).

43. See Berard Marthaler, "The Modern Catechetical Movement in Roman Catholicism" in *Sourcebook for Modern Catechetic,* ed. Michael Warren, 279 (Winona: Saint Mary's Press, 1983).

44. Marthaler, "The Modern Catechetical Movement in Roman Catholicism" 279.

45. Marthaler, "The Modern Catechetical Movement in Roman Catholicism" 279.

46. *General Directory for Catechesis*, no.21.

47. *General Directory for Catechesis*, no.30.

48. *National Directory for Catechesis*, no.19, sect A.

49. *National Directory for Catechesis*, no. 47.

50. *National Directory for Catechesis,* no. 48, sect A.

51. *National Directory for Catechesis,* no. 48, sect A.

52. *National Directory for Catechesis,* no. 48, sect A.

53. *National Directory for Catechesis,* no. 48, sect A-1.

54. *National Directory for Catechesis,* no. 48, sect A-2.

55. *National Directory for Catechesis,* no. 48, sect A-3.

56. *National Directory for Catechesis*, no. 48, sect A-3.

57. *National Directory for Catechesis*, no. 48, sect A-4.

58. *National Directory for Catechesis*, no. 48, sect A-4.

59. *National Directory for Catechesis*, no. 48, sect A-4.

60. *National Directory for Catechesis,* no. 19, sect. D.

61. *National Directory for Catechesis,* no. 19, sect. D.

62. *National Directory for Catechesis*, no. 19, sect. D.

63. *National Directory for Catechesis*, no. 19, sect. E.

64. *National Directory for Catechesis*, no. 19, sect. E.

65. *National Directory for Catechesis*, no. 48.

66. *National Directory for Catechesis*, no. 48.

67. *National Directory for Catechesis*, no. 48, sect. E-2.

68. *Sharing the Light of Faith: National Catechetical Directory for Catholics of the United States.* (United States Catholic Conference, Department of Education, 1979) no.175.

69. *National Directory for Catechesis*, no. 48, sect. D.

70. Thomas Groome, "Parish as Catechist" in *Church,* Fall, 1990, 24.

71. *National Directory for Catechesis,* no. 19, sect. C.

72. *National Directory for Catechesis*, no. 19, sect. C.

73. *National Directory for Catechesis*, no. 19, sect. C.

74. *National Directory for Catechesis*, no. 29, sect. C.

75. *National Directory for Catechesis*, no. 29, sect. C.

76. *National Directory for Catechesis*, no. 29, sect. C.

77. *National Directory for Catechesis*, no. 29, sect. C.

78. *National Directory for Catechesis*, no. 29, sect. D.

79. *National Directory for Catechesis*, no. 29, sect. D.

80. *National Directory for Catechesis,* no. 29, sect. D.

81. *National Directory for Catechesis,* no. 53.

82. *National Directory for Catechesis*, no. 53.

83. *National Directory for Catechesis*, no. 54, sect. A.

84. *National Directory for Catechesis*, no. 54, sect. A.

85. *National Directory for Catechesis*, no. 54, sect. B.

86. *National Directory for Catechesis*, no. 54, sect. B-2.

87. *National Directory for Catechesis*, no. 54, sect. B-2.

88. *National Directory for Catechesis*, no. 54, sect. B-2.

89. *National Directory for Catechesis*, no. 54, sect. B-3.

90. *National Directory for Catechesis,* no. 54, sect. B-4.

91. *National Directory for Catechesis*, no. 54, sect. B-5.

92. *National Directory for Catechesis*, no. 54, sect. B-5.

93. *National Directory for Catechesis*, no. 54, sect. B-6.

94. *National Directory for Catechesis*, no. 54, sect. B-7.

95. *National Directory for Catechesis*, no. 54, sect. B-7.

96. *National Directory for Catechesis*, no. 54, sect. B-8.

97. *National Directory for Catechesis*, no. 54, sect. B-8.

98. *National Directory for Catechesis*, no. 54, sect. B-8.

99. *National Directory for Catechesis*, no. 54, sect. B-9.

100. *National Directory for Catechesis,* no. 54, sect. B-9.

101. *National Directory for Catechesis,* no. 54, sect. B-9.

102. *National Directory for Catechesis,* no. 54, sect. B-9.

103. *National Directory for Catechesis,* no. 54, sect. C.

104. *National Directory for Catechesis,* no. 54, sect. C.

105. *National Directory for Catechesis,* no. 55, sect. B.

106. *National Directory for Catechesis,* no. 55, sect. B.

107. *National Directory for Catechesis,* no. 55, sect. C.

108. *National Directory for Catechesis,* no. 54, sect. A.

109. *National Directory for Catechesis,* no. 54, sect. B.

110. *National Directory for Catechesis,* no. 55, sect. F.

111. *National Directory for Catechesis,* no. 28.

112. *National Directory for Catechesis,* no. 28, sect. A-1,2,3,4 and B.

113. *National Directory for Catechesis,* no. 28, sect. B.

114. *National Directory for Catechesis,* no. 28, sect. B.

115. *National Directory for Catechesis,* no. 28, sect. B.

116. *National Directory for Catechesis,* no. 28, sect. B.

117. *National Directory for Catechesis,* no. 29.

118. *National Directory for Catechesis,* no. 29.

119. *National Directory for Catechesis,* no. 29.

120. *National Directory for Catechesis,* no. 29.

121. *National Directory for Catechesis,* no. 35, sect. D.

122. *National Directory for Catechesis,* no. 35, sect. D.

123. *National Directory for Catechesis,* no. 29, sect. A-H.

124. *National Directory for Catechesis,* no. 32.

125. *National Directory for Catechesis,* no. 33.

126. *National Directory for Catechesis,* no. 33.

127. *National Directory for Catechesis,* no. 31.

128. *National Directory for Catechesis,* no. 24, sect. B.

129. *National Directory for Catechesis,* no. 24, sect. C.

130. *National Directory for Catechesis,* no. 24, sect. C.

131. *National Directory for Catechesis,* no. 25, sect. A.

132. *National Directory for Catechesis,* no. 25, sect. C.

133. *National Directory for Catechesis,* no. 25, sect. C.

134. *National Directory for Catechesis,* no. 28, sect. A.

135. *National Directory for Catechesis,* no. 25, sect. B.

136. See Catherine M. La Cugna, *God for Us: The Trinity and Christian Life.* (San Francisco: Harper), 1991.

137. *National Directory for Catechesis,* no.8.

138. *National Directory for Catechesis,* no. 8.

139. *National Directory for Catechesis,* no. 25, sect. D.

140. *National Directory for Catechesis,* no. 24, sect. C.

141. *National Directory for Catechesis,* no. 41, sect A.

142. *National Directory for Catechesis,* no. 41, sect A.

143. *National Directory for Catechesis,* no. 41, sect A.

144. *National Directory for Catechesis,* no. 42.

Chapter Four

Contemporary Theory
in Religious Education

INTRODUCTION

In Chapter Two, the history of religious education in the United States was explored from its Protestant beginnings to the establishment of the Religious Education Association (1903), and the Religious Education Movement that birthed the term *religious education*. From approximately 1935 to 1965, neo-orthodoxy theology reigned supreme and the shift to *Christian education* contracted the parameters of the field. However, the search for a new meaning and identity of religious education began to take hold during the period 1965 to 1975.

This search for a new meaning and identity of religious education during the 1970's is recounted in a work edited by John Westerhoff titled: *Who Are We? The Quest For a Religious Education.* In the introduction, Westerhoff describes the state of religious education during this time:

> For some seventy-two years *Religious Education* has been the voice of similar folk. Except, however, for the earliest years, when those who made up its membership shared a clear sense of purpose, the association has experienced one identity crisis after another, though today's appears to be the worst. Even the names used to identify its constituency have continually changed, though with the exception of the gradual addition of women, blacks, Roman Catholics, Jews, and Canadians, the membership has remained essentially older liberal intellectuals. While the name of the association and the journal has been constant throughout the years, you will find in the journal the words religious education, religious instruction, Christian (Jewish) education, Christian nurture, Christian instruction, church (synagogue) education, ecumenical education, and catechesis. Though the name religious education has been used most

frequently, there has been no complete or consistent agreement on what those words mean or what they refer. Today there is less concurrence than ever before. While always in search of an identity, today we can not even agree on a name by which to be identified.[1]

More than thirty-three years have passed since Westerhoff's observations and the quest for clarity and identity of the field has continued. This chapter is concerned with the re-founding and development of the field of religious education during the past thirty years (1975-2005).

Methodically, the task of exploring the emerging meaning of religious education follows a parallel path to the five themes pertaining to catechesis in the previous chapter. So, the five particular corresponding themes as related to religious education will be addressed.

It should be noted that the titles of the themes themselves propose similarities and differences between catechesis and religious education, connoting that each field has its own language. The themes in relation to religious education are: 1) the meaning and identity of contemporary religious education; 2) the meaning of religious maturity; 3) the context of contemporary religious education; 4) educational methodologies in contemporary religious education; and 5) the religious foundations of contemporary religious education. Through the exploration of these themes, as was done with catechesis, this chapter will address the "what," "where," "who," "when," "how," and "why" of contemporary religious education.

These themes will be examined through the works of significant religious education theorists such as Maria Harris, Kieran Scott, and in particular, the writings of Gabriel Moran. The meaning and identity of contemporary religious education will be dealt with first.

THE MEANING AND IDENTITY OF
CONTEMPORARY RELIGIOUS EDUCATION

The need for a contemporary meaning and identity of religious education is evident when the historical roots of the field are tracked. The original vision of *religious education,* namely, "To inspire the educational forces of our country with the religious ideal; to inspire the religious forces of our country with the educational ideal; and to keep before the public mind the idea of Religious Education and the sense of its need and value",[2] has struggled from its inception to stay intact.

Today the field of religious education continues to struggle as it attempts to find identity and meaning in a post-modern world. As noted above, terms used for the identification of religious education have changed. The use of the term interchangeably with other forms of church/synagogue education has added to confusion in the field. This is problematic also for John Westerhoff. He writes: "The matter of a name is more than semantics. Each possible name reflects some distinctive variance in our understanding of who we are and what we are to be about."[3]

The need for a new language and meaning of religious education has been pioneered, in particular, by Gabriel Moran. As a theorist of contemporary religious education, Moran's work emerges as a significant challenge to religious education as synonymous with what church communities do to transmit their faith to a younger generation.[4] His work is a shift of paradigm beyond Christian Education and catechesis. He attempts to reclaim and re-conceptualize the original meaning of the term *religious education*. In doing so, he ushers us into a whole new field of endeavor.[5]

The Paradigm Shift of Gabriel Moran

For Gabriel Moran, the meaning of the term *religious education* has been domesticated in the Christian churches. Christianity can contribute to its meaning, he notes, but Christianity does not own it; there is more to the functioning meaning of religious education than ecclesial thought control of children. What is needed, he claims, is the intersection of religion and education. Here religion would challenge the quality and purpose of all education, and education would challenge existing religious institutions with the test of education.[6]

In 1974, Moran viewed Christian theology and religious education as paralyzed within a language of the Reformation period. He observed:

> Religious education is everywhere deficient and Christianity could make an important contribution to improve it. But Christianity's contribution is knowledge and practice, not faith. To the extent that faith connotes a positive human attitude it, underlies all religious education but is not in the special possession of any group. Knowledge and practice do differ from one group to another and are also capable of being shared . . . People are leaving the church in search of sacraments, mystical prayer and religious community. If church theology and history were presented as something other than victory communiqués, people might find that there was more to their religion than what is subsumed under the term Christian faith. Perhaps many of us have to go around the world to come home again, but the journey would be less traumatic if there were a linguistic and communal setting in which we might experience a human way of living, dying and going beyond dying.[7]

Moran suggests that such an upheaval could not be contained within the Christian church of the time. Thus he calls for the rediscovery of imagination, metaphor, and symbolism in daily living that could form the basis of a new religious language, the creation of a new field of religious education, and a reshaped meaning of the term *religious education.*

Moran offers three principles for this reshaped meaning of religious education: 1) religious education pertains to all of life and to all education. Here, religious education, in the short term, is that protest against the closure of life, education and imagination, and a protest that no finite thing is god; 2) religious education, at its best, is accomplished through the artistic and cultic. Here the use of ritual, symbols, and gestures gives calm in a world filled with chaos. This is the most powerful form of religious education; and 3) religious education in the Christian church ought to be not a study of faith but a way of knowledge. This would entail a carefully structured set of experiences that could issue in a path of knowledge and techniques.[8]

The Two Languages of Religious Education

If there is to be a reshaping or reforming of r*eligious education,* it needs to be examined within the context in which it finds its meaning. As Moran sees it, there are, in fact, two contexts: ecclesiastical and educational. These two contexts, in turn, give rise to the two current languages of religious education. While ecclesial language is concrete, it contains the danger of parochialism. Educational language, on the other hand, is amorphous and needs the concreteness that churches, synagogues, and other religious organizations can bring to it. One should not abandon one for the other. Moran warns that religious education should not be reduced to the language of the Church. The Catholic tradition does this when it equates *catechesis* with *religious education.* The Protestant tradition repeats the same mistake when it interchanges *religious education* with the term *Christian Education.* Moran's fundamental premise, however, is that *religious education* "is etymologically, historically, and operationally wider in meaning than catechetics or Christian Education."[9]

For example, the relationship of theology to catechetics and Christian Education determines the ecclesiastical language of religious education. Only an approved theology is allowed to enter into the content of catechesis and Christian Education. Therefore, the ecclesial form of religious education has two components: 1) theology and 2) catechetics/Christian Education. However, Moran suggests that theology, while it dictates the content to be used, stands outside the discussion of religious education; there is more to education than a body of content. "Catechetics," Moran states, "therefore, cannot dialogue with theology because theology controls the language. The way to open a dialogue within the churches is to place the study of religion into an educational rather than ecclesiastical context."[10] This, for the most part, is what the Christian churches fail to do.

On the other hand, Moran suggests that educational establishments can be just as narrow and rigid as religious organizations. Education, meaning the systemic planning of experience for growth and human understanding, can be taken over by schools in a way that is similar to the church's control of religion. Schools are only one means to promote education; church, family, and work also are educationally important. Within education, religious issues can surface anywhere. "Religion exists," he writes, "not simply as mental construct but as personal attitude, communal symbol and bodily behavior."[11] Therefore, religion should be brought into the educational arena.

Education is concerned with bringing ordinary experience under control. It heightens the rational, the controlling element of experience. Religion, on the other hand, breaks out of the ordinary, the ordered, controlled, and fixed. It is logical, then, that religion and education are in tension with one another. Moran explains:

> Religion and education are like a bickering couple who don't get along well together but who are worse off when apart. The near impossibility of religious education might be a consolation for those in the work. The closer one gets to a real religious education, the greater becomes the tension between the two words.[12]

Although he recognizes and acknowledges this tension, Moran suggests that the educational setting is capable of having religious significance. In other words, the religious can emerge from within education and permeate its practice. Let us now turn to the principles suggested by Moran for such an occurrence to take place.

Three Principles for an Emerging Field

For Moran, there are three principles of a full context for education in religion. These components are: 1) the study of a specific religion from within; 2) the study of religion from a position of some distance; and 3) the practice of a religious life.[13]

1) The study of religion from within is concerned with an appreciation of things for their own unique selves. This does not imply introversion or defensiveness but it entails the acknowledgement that religious institutions are to be appreciated on their own terms. This implies that the religious in religious education has to be concrete, and particular. Included is the ability to get inside a tradition and to understand its particular form of language. An educational setting in which to work intelligently, patiently, and reverently

is needed to carry out such a task. For example, the scriptures, ecclesiastical history, and tradition should be studied with patient detail and in a scholarly fashion.

2) The study of religion from a distance is the second component for a full religious education. This would mean stepping back from involvement in one religion to consider its relation to other religious and nonreligious choices. Such an event would provide a greater appreciation of one's own religious life and less misunderstanding of other people's. A stronger confirmation in one's own religious tradition occurs when people of different religious backgrounds meet in an educational setting. However, in isolation from the others, this component would be inadequate and perhaps destructive. Therefore, the study of religion from a distance is crucial to the whole undertaking.[14]

For Moran, the public sector of education is the obvious place to engage in this form of religious education. While the study of religion in the public schools of the United States is legally possible and educationally desirable, the absence of a language to discuss religion as a normal part of public education is problematic. The task of teaching religion, however, can be explosive. But Moran queries, "If religion in institutions set aside for education is not examined, where can this process take place?"

Public school is where the majority of children (including Roman Catholics) are educated. It is the public school, he suggests, where religion ought to be part of education, if only to make the school more public. However, Moran concludes that while the teaching of religion in the school setting is an indispensable part of religious education in the contemporary world, this form of teaching cannot sustain a religious life on its own. Other educational life forms also play a part in preserving, continuing and enriching the religious life. He advises that educational theorists might profitably examine, in the light of religious history, whether they might be missing the larger picture of education.[15]

3) The third component, the practice of a religious life, can be summarized as: prayer and social action. This part of religious education, not studied or taught directly but indirectly, calls for an element of privacy or intimacy. There is a time to study elements of a religion and a time to practice religion. For Moran, practice belongs at the center of education. Some of the practices that Christian churches can bring to enhance education include the contemplative, the sacramental, and the protest against injustice.[16]

The total process of religious education should provide a place for passing on the past. This work can be done through non-verbal ritual and through the study of history in order to hand over the wisdom of the last generation to the next. Moran offers a meaning of religious education that would save what we most value from our past but would open new doors for the future. He writes:

A good distinction does not destroy any of the past though it may chasten our claims about past and present. In the past we may have spoken as if we alone had the truth. The challenge now of religious education is to help us speak and live the truth we know while also removing the intolerance which is embedded in our language. To any other person or group we can then say: Here is our way. Show us your way.[17]

With these early proposals, Moran advocates a meaning of religious education as the intersection of religion and education in its multiple forms in multiple settings. While these suggestions of Moran's may offer material for conversation, can they be too idealistic in light of the contemporary state of public schooling and religious institutions? In other words, are public school institutions and religious institutions ready to submit to such an ideal? Could educational leaders be open to such an enterprise? Would religious leaders be willing to cooperate on terms that might force them to acquiesce control in areas of content and/or methodology? How and where would teachers of religion in public schools be educated and trained? Would religious institutions agree to such an endeavor? And, finally, would religious institutions open themselves to the challenge and critique of education?

The Four Qualities of a New Religious Education Conversation

If religious education has to do with the religious life of the human race and with bringing people within the influence of that life, the premise for this is a wider conversation. What would such a conversation entail?

Moran recognizes that there is no preordained endpoint to such conversation, for all good conversation is endless.[18] However, a wider religious education conversation would not include proselytizing or indoctrination. Nor would it explain away a religion. Moran suggests four guidelines for such a conversation. It needs to be: 1) international; 2) interreligious; 3) intergenerational; and 4) interinstitutional.

1) International Conversation

In contemporary times, every field of study needs to take account of what is happening worldwide. Religious education is no different. It is closely related to national governments, and many religions cut across national lines. Such conversation is challenging since the term *religious education* has no exact equivalent in many languages. Such is the case, for example, with England and the United States. In the former, religious education usually means a subject in the curriculum of a state school. In the latter, religion is not taught in public schools, and therefore, it becomes more ecclesial and familial, rather than a schooling enterprise.[19] Such a babel of languages, with interchangeability of terms, and multiple meanings, has caused an identity crisis for the field of religious education and the role of religious educators. The absence of a consistent and comprehensive theory that includes philosophical assumptions and foundational principles adds to the chaos.[20] In spite of these challenges, Moran finds that there are many similarities as well as startling differences between countries in their concern for religious education. Conversations without end are needed in order to discover where true agreements and disagreements are positioned. Such an endeavor may unfold meanings that could be incorporated into in a comprehensive theory.

2) Interreligious Conversation

The interreligious aspect of religious education is inherent to religious education itself. The religious has multiple forms and diversity. Today, religious groups and individuals within each group find themselves in a world of religious pluralism. Unlike a survey of the world religions, an interreligious approach is one that promotes the understanding of one's own religious position in relation to other religious possibilities. To avoid the circumstance that one religion would assert itself as superior, suppressing others, or not take other religions seriously, religious pluralism today demands that each religion be affirmed as important but only in relation to others. Such an enterprise would fail unless there is genuine education within each group and between groups. "Thus," states Moran, "religious pluralism has been the condition that led to religious education, but religious education is the condition for sustaining religious pluralism."[21] A Christian, Jewish, or Muslim, religious education is concerned with the history, teachings, and ritual of each. How each of these elements is approached determines "whether the process is really educational or whether it is an attempt to fix the mind on an established body of material that bears no further development."[22] Moran explains:

> Without a religious group having to retract its belief in the way, the truth, and the life, there can be acknowledgement that other people have a particular way, truth, and life. The opposite of a logically true statement is a logically false statement; the opposite of a religious way of life can be another religious way of life.[23]

3) Intergenerational Conversation

The term *intergenerational* implies that we are being taught all the time by those who are younger and those older than ourselves. Religious education can aid in the conversation of generations. It runs from birth to death. Conversation between the living generations also is a reminder of a larger conversation with one's ancestors, with nonhuman life and the voice of creation. Religious education can remind the rest of education to include the relation of the very old and the very young.[24] The old and the young have a natural alliance that needs to be realized. Moran suggests that younger children and older adults may have a profound religious sense, something that needs to be preserved throughout the hurriedness of middle age. In a word, religious education is life-long.

4) Interinstitutional Conversation

Interinstitutional education is a geographical interplay of human organization. Educational life forms in this ecology are: a) family (community); b) schooling (literate knowledge); c) job (work); and d) leisure (contemplative wisdom). "These forms of education," states Moran, "are simply the main places where the reshaping of life occurs in relation to human purpose."[25] Each is a distinctive form of education, and each may come to the center of our life at different periods in our life. More in-depth descriptions of the settings for these forms will be presented later in this chapter.

Both the state and the religious body have a similar relation to all four forms. The former is to provide good economic and social conditions and the latter is to provide examples of community, work, knowledge and wisdom.[26]

a) The family is the first educational agent that one is exposed to. It is within the family where each member learns and is influenced by the relational dynamics of the others. This educational agent is a most important and influential educational life form for the members within and for the larger community without.

b) The function of the school as an educational life form is to provide a place for intellectual knowledge. It provides a zone of intellectual freedom where all questions can be asked including difficult questions concerning the contemporary world. However, the school cannot stand alone in this endeavor. Moran explains:

> Interinstitutional religious education becomes actual as education is understood to include not only the form of schooling but the other three forms . . . Schooling can be helpful for adults, but it needs to be integrated with the other three forms . . . Religious education will then be seen to emerge at the center of education not at the periphery.[27]

c) An individual's job allows one to contribute to society. However, participating in non-job related work also gives one purpose. Liturgy and service programs can remind people of a deeper meaning of work.

d) Retirement offers a time and place for wisdom to emerge. However, wisdom needs to be present in quiet moments elsewhere in life. We are educated by rest, silence, and contemplation. Religious bodies ought to provide a refuge of contemplative quiet in an increasingly noisy world.

The Aims of Religious Education

In the quest for a renewed meaning and identity of religious education, it is essential to understand its aims. Moran claims that religious education has two distinct and equally important aims. These aims are held in tension with one another. The two aims are: 1) teaching people to be religious in a particular way and 2) teaching people religion. The first aim has as its object the practice of one concrete set of activities that excludes other ways of acting. The second aim is to understand religion as an area of scholarly interest, an academic subject. [28]

Whatever the situation, the aims of religious education are to be intact and clear if they are to be accomplished. They also need to be in dialogue with each other if the term *religious education* is to be fully recognized. The formation of life within a community and an intellectual understanding are to be embraced by a religious education.[29]

There may be a time in one's life, or in one's day, to focus on one aim or the other. Eventually, both aims will come together in the person of the learner. It is the mature adult who can hold these two aims in fruitful tension.

Although the topic of teaching will be explored in more detail later in this chapter, it should be acknowledged that for Moran, teaching is one of the most important and regular acts that humans perform in life. Actually, a deeper and wider meaning for teaching is necessary in order for the first aim of religious education to be understood and met. Moran declares in sum: "religious education means teaching people religion with all the breadth and depth of intellectual excitement one is capable of—and teaching people to be religious with the particularity of the verbal and nonverbal symbols that place us along one path of life."[30]

With this new framework, Moran's work represents an attempt to retrieve and to re-conceptualize the richest meaning of the term *religious education.* The vision here is to transcend the local ecclesial community without negating it, and to meet religious issues in an educationally appropriate way. This re-conceptualized religious education is a more mature form of religious education. Kieran Scott explains:

> There is a fundamental truth in the reconceptualized form of religious education . . . This educational process enables us to step out of our own parochial mind-

set, ideology and identity and pass over to other standpoints, values and truths. This journey sets us on a corporate search for truth, value and identity. It will lead to the reconstruction of our religious imagination and the expansion of the horizon of our tradition.[31]

However, every enterprise has its limitations and this re-conceptualized form of religious education is no different. Scott offers some thought to the limitations of this paradigm. First, religious education is largely undeveloped in practice and there has been no acquired allegiance of professional educators in this regard. Second, this form is in danger of remaining ideational and lacking historical grounding. It remains to be embodied in a fully developed curriculum or programmatic form. The structure and nature of an accredited degree in religious education in light of this new scope, form, and purpose, present their own set of questions. Third, catechists and Christian religious educators find it difficult to identify with the re-conceptualist form of religious education. They remain knowledgeable and loyal to their own particular traditions. Finally, Scott notes, "The paradigmatic shift required seems unnecessary or, at least, to risk too much. It could lead to the deconstruction of firmly held tenets in their religious traditions."[32]

Since it is in its infancy stage, it remains to be seen if a re-conceptualist form of religious education can overcome the obstacles that may keep it from maturation.

THE MEANING OF RELIGIOUS MATURITY IN RELIGIOUS EDUCATION

The field of religious education, like the field of catechesis, acknowledges that growth in faith is related to human development and is developed by the passage through particular stages.[33] The catechetical documents, of the United States, however, warn that catechesis is not to be linked with a single explanation of the stages of human development. These documents also do not name any authors/theorists associated with growth in faith as related to human development. However, some catechetical theorists do recognize the scholarship that human developmentalists have contributed to the understanding of the roles of faith and maturity in the process of religious learning.[34] Religious education theorists outside the Roman Catholic establishment acknowledge this scholarship as well, although it is significant to note there are similarities and differences in their approaches. With this in mind, it is appropriate to now turn to the constructs of a number of these theorists. We begin with the most prominent, the work of James W. Fowler.

James Fowler and Stages of Faith Development

James W. Fowler is one who has emerged as a proponent of faith development. He identifies seven stages of faith development based on: 1) his synthesis of Jean Piaget's, Lawrence Kohlberg's, and Erik Erikson's stage theories; and 2) more than four hundred interviews with adults and children. H. Richard Neibuhr and Paul Tillich provide the theological sources for his work. The word *faith* in the title of his book, *Stages of Faith: The Psychology of Human Development and the Quest for Meaning,* reflects Fowler's broad understanding of faith as that which gives meaning and purpose to our lives.[35]

Fowler's understanding of faith includes the following: 1) Faith, rather than belief or religion, is the most fundamental category in the human quest for relation to transcendence; 2) Each of the major religious traditions speaks about faith in ways that make the same phenomenon visible; 3) Faith is an orientation of the total person, giving purpose and goal to one's hopes and strivings, thoughts and actions; 4) The unity and recognizability of faith, despite the myriad variants of religion and beliefs, support the struggle to maintain and develop a theory of religious relativity in which the religions—and the faith they evoke and shape—are seen as relative apprehensions of our relatedness to that which is universal.[36]

Fowler bases the evolution of a pre-stage and six subsequent stages of faith development on the optimal relations between psychosocial development and the structural-developmental stages of faith. This basis may help to clarify in what sense faith stages may be said to be normative.[37] He describes the term *stage* as "an integrated set of operational structures that constitute the thought processes of a person at a given time."[38] *Development* for Fowler involves "the transformation of such 'structures of the whole' in the direction of greater internal differentiation, complexity and stability."[39] A stage transition occurs when a novelty or challenge emerges that cannot be assimilated into an existing structure or stage and when enough accommodation has been undertaken to require a transformation.[40] We turn now to describe Fowler's stages of faith development.

Pre-stage—*Undifferentiated faith* (from birth to age 2)—Here "the seeds of trust, courage, hope and love are fused in an undifferentiated way and contend with sensed threats of abandonment, inconsistencies and deprivations in an infant's environment."[41] The quality of mutuality, the strength of trust, autonomy, hope and courage developed in this phase underlie or threaten to determine all that comes later in faith development.

Stage 1—*Intuitive-Projective Faith* (ages 2-6)—Cognitive egocentrism, a predominance of fantasy, and a lack of logic predominate the thinking of children at this age. The birth of emergent imagination and the ability to unify and grasp the experience-world are the strengths of this stage. Dangers of this stage arise from "the possible 'possession' of the child's imagination by unrestrained images of terror and destructiveness, or from the witting or unwitting exploitation of her or his imagination in the reinforcement of taboos and moral or doctrinal expectations."[42]

Stage 2—*Mythic-literal Faith* (ages 6/7- 11/12)—children at this stage begin to take on for themselves the stories, beliefs and observations that symbolize belonging to their communities. Beliefs, moral rules, and attitudes are appropriated with literal interpretations. Narrative and the emergence of story, drama, and myth arise as ways of finding and giving coherence to experience. Literalness and an excessive reliance on reciprocity for constructing an ultimate environment can be limiting.[43]

Stage 3—*Synthetic-Conventional Faith* (ages 11/12—17/18 or later)—The forming of a personal myth of one's own becoming in identity and faith emerges that can provide a coherent means of navigating a complex world beyond the family. Dependence on the views, expectations, and evaluations of others emerges during this stage. Beliefs are typically inhabited rather than being subjected to critical reflection. Interpersonal betrayals can give rise to nihilistic despair.[44]

Stage 4—*Individuative-Reflective Faith* (young adulthood or later)—During this stage, the self now claims an identity that is no longer defined by the composite of one's roles or meanings to others; self (identity) and outlook (world view) are differentiated from those of others. Symbols are translated into conceptual meanings and the capacity for critical reflection on identity and outlook emerges. A danger here can be " . . . an excessive confidence in the conscious mind and in critical thought and a kind of second narcissism in which the now clearly bounded, reflective self overassimilates 'reality' and the perspective of others into its own world view."[45]

Stage 5—*Conjunctive Faith* (midlife)—Persons in this stage develop what Paul Ricoeur named, a "second naivete" described as symbolic power reunited with conceptual meanings. There also is a new reclaiming and reworking of one's past and a listening to the voices of one's deeper self. Also involved is a critical recognition of one's social unconscious encompassing the myths, ideal images and prejudices that are built deeply into the self-system. A paradox remains, for the stage five person, between living and acting in an untransformed world while maintaining transforming vision and sustaining loyalties. In some cases, this division lures persons toward radical actualization that is a part of Stage 6.[46]

Stage 6—*Universalizing Faith*—For Fowler, this stage represents a culminating image of mature faith.[47] Fowler recognizes that this stage is extremely rare. He offers Gandhi, Martin Luther King, Jr., Mother Teresa of Calcutta, Dag Hammarskjöld, Dietrich Bonhoeffer, Abraham Heschel, and Thomas Merton as representatives of Stage 6.

Fowler's work causes Felicity B. Kelcourse to acknowledge that Fowler provides a way to think of faith that "transcends the narrow confines of particular religions traditions and can therefore contribute in useful ways to ecumenical, international, and intercultural dialogue."[48]

His work, however, has come under criticism from religious educators, in particular, Gabriel Moran. We now turn to Moran's critique of Fowler's faith development scheme and his alternative proposal for a pattern of religious development and religious maturity.

Gabriel Moran on the Faith Development Theory of James W. Fowler

Gabriel Moran shares Fowler's concern that there is a lack of attention to the spiritual, religious, and faith journeys of persons in today's secular world, including the world of educational institutions. He agrees that there is a need to explore a "logic of conviction" not reducible to the behavioral sciences' concern for the logic of certainty. At this point, Moran departs from Fowler. He questions 1) if there a need of another theory of development and 2) specifically, Fowler's intention of constructing a theory of faith development.[49]

In choosing the term *faith development,* Moran sees Fowler as attempting to: 1) build a bridge between the secular world and the world of religious traditions; and 2) build a bridge between the many religious traditions that use a word that corresponds to the term *faith.* He is uncertain if either bridge has been successfully built by *faith development.* Efforts in this direction, Moran claims, may be unsuccessful due to Fowler's use of the term *faith.*[50] Actually Moran is concerned with the terms *faith, development,* and *stage* that dominate Fowler's work. We now examine the basis for Moran's concern(s).

Fowler's use of the term *human faith* contrasts with any other kind of faith and instead of overcoming a dichotomy it threatens to do the opposite. It also may exclude a religious meaning to faith that Moran believes to be an unwise choice. He explains:

> Faith in its richest, most important meaning is not an object or a human pos-
> session. It is a gift to which a human being responds. As the applicability of
> the word *faith* widens (a movement that Fowler approves), the breadth of its
> meaning narrows (a movement that Fowler disregards). From the standpoint
> of Jewish, Christian, or Muslim traditions the most focused meaning of faith

involves one simple issue: Have you accepted God's gift? Are you on God's side, or the devil's? The harsh language in each group dividing the work into "the faithful" and "the infidels" is an inevitable result of the logic of faith. The danger comes when a group presumes that it can infallibly draw the line between the faithful and the infidels. Jewish, Christian and Muslim traditions at their most self-critical agree on this point: Only God knows for sure who is on God's side.[51]

In addition, Moran believes there should be an inner tension of several meanings of believing and a healthy tension between faith and the religious aspects of believing, tensions that appear to be omitted by Fowler. "Our world," states Moran, "needs to be linked back into religious sources through its beliefs . . . Instead of severing faith and belief, we need to be working out the intricate web of meanings within faith."[52]

A metaphor of *development,* for Moran, transcends the scientific fields. He suggests the need of an image of development that "avoids both a predetermined endpoint and a stifling biological determinism."[53] Moran's thoughts and suggestions about this will be examined later in this section.

Moran is also concerned whether the Piagetian-style theory of dealing with *stages,* that is seminal to Fowler's work, is an appropriate way to describe a journey of faith. In this context, a separation of the *how* and *what* is observed by Moran, noting that Piagetian structure has little reference to content terms. In other words, he is more concerned with whether the issue should be about a meaning of faith that would include the meaning of hope, love, revelation, grace, and other religious categories rather than about the *structure* of faith.[54]

Moran credits Fowler with attempting to heal this separation of structure and content. However, while the structure of faith can be studied in the life of a person of any religious affiliation, the content, by which such persons live is obscured, at least temporarily. A separation of structure and content causes a concern for Moran as to whether structure and content as separate elements can mean anything religiously. Therefore, unless the content is brought somewhere back in the theory, the description of *stages* can be limiting in the context of religious development.[55] For Moran, Fowler's six stages of faith development are in need of an imagery that keeps turning the question of an end back into the process itself. Religious imagery, not simply the *content,* serves to guide and transform each stage of life.[56]

Gabriel Moran's Proposal of Religious Development

In offering an alternative proposal, Moran's focus of concern is not about structures of faith but about the composite of religious factors among which there are several meanings of faith. He uses the term *stage* not to mean a movement up a hierarchy of stages. Rather, he writes, they are "stages of religious development (that) proceed with a circling back that creates a spiraling effect."[57] Moran offers three stages, with two moments within each, of religious development and correlates them with Fowler's six stages. This correlation is:

1) *Simply Religious*—correlates to Fowler's pre-stage and some of #1 and #2.
2) *Acquiring a Religion*—correlates to Fowler's #1 and #2; Also all of #3 and #4.
3) *The Religiously Christian (Jewish, Muslim, and so forth)*—correlates to Fowler's #5 and #6.

Within each of the three stages, Moran acknowledges two moments that are specific to each. We now turn to these stages and their specificities.

1) *Simply religious*—birth (or even a few months before) to ages 5-7. This stage is distinguished by the physical and the mythic. The former (the first physical moment of this stage) acknowledges the infant/child's dependency on the physical affection and care provided by others and the child's eventual attempt to separate from the parent. These moments evoke a step toward interdependence between both parent and child. This period of life, from a religious standpoint, signifies two life lessons: 1) whatever good we have is a gift, not a right, and 2) the realization that we are part of a community that reflects we are saved in, by, and through other persons. The notion that the divine is everywhere, manifested in life's daily miracles, indicates the mystery and wonder present in the religious life of the child. The latter (second mythical moment of this stage) is a stage of bright imagery and powerful stories. Religious experience for the child can be joyful as well as terrifying. This dualism dominates the child's mind in the form of good versus evil and the struggle of life and death. The religious life of the child at this stage is marked by the desire to be on the side of life.

2) *Acquiring a religion*—ages 5/6 to adolescence. The two movements within this stage are: our people's beliefs and, disbeliefs. The first movement of this stage is marked by the child's questions and search for answers in order to come to terms with the mysteries of the universe. At first the answers received from parents, teachers and trusted adults satisfy the child because they are "our people's beliefs." Knowledge of such beliefs provides identification with a particular people who have a past and who are shaping a future. The young person eventually must deal with increased realities and soon begins to dismantle the belief system that has been built. Moran names this movement "disbelief" that is directed at the verbal, external side of faith.

The upheaval caused by the independence/dependence issues of childhood calls for a place where young people can rebel against their upbringing while they hold on to their underlying love of family and friends.

3) *Religiously Christian (Jewish, Muslim, etc)*—post-adolescence to adulthood—during this stage of religious development, the adult no longer has a religion, so to speak, but is religious in a particular way. While "having a religion" can be good, it is not good enough according to Moran. Not only does a religious person recognize her/his own religion, she/he also appreciates other particular religious persons. What is shared is a common religious quest in spite of differences in a religious particularity. Moran names the first movement of the stage "parable" since during this time, the adult reflects on life's paradoxes and iniquities. This is the time when one recognizes that the search for answers must go on. The earlier experiences of life are now brought into tension with the present. Moran explains:

> The infant's sense of unity, the child's sense of duality, and the adolescent's sense of rational system all come together in adult religiousness. Religious language is now understood to be not a set of sacred words or a collection of texts or sacred objects but a process of using language to subvert our conceptions of the ordinary world and reveal a deeper truth. In adolescence, the role of storyteller is diminished . . . In adulthood, life itself is understood as a story, and fiction is now seen as sometimes more revealing than fact . . . A parabolic outlook gives one a sense of belonging to a specific group and a particular history. The religious adult appeals to "my people" as an embodiment of "the people." The beliefs of our people can now function not as blinders to a wider truth but as powerful stimuli to act on behalf of all.[58]

The parabolic attitude is never left behind but is enriched by the development of a contemplative center to life. This attitude shades into the final movement of religious development and is identified by Moran as *detachment*. It is at this time when one is finally detached from everything, including one's own life. Being detached entails the willingness to wait and to possess the determination and the patience to stay with what one determines to be her/his call in life. After doing the best one can do, she/he takes no credit but gives glory to the source of all gifts. This is a time of movement toward deeper communion and toward the heart of reality. It is the time when all of life's elements are synthesized as one prepares for a new birth, namely, death.[59]

Moran assumes that the characteristic of detachment is common in later life; an assumption that differs from Fowler's reservation that this is characteristic for a few mystical souls.

Perhaps the third stage of being *Religiously Christian* et al. is the most significant for Moran in light of the concept of religious maturity. In summary, it is during this time that 1) sufficient experience and a degree of openness bring about a reintegration of one's relation to the universe; 2) there is an acceptance of diversity within unity, allowing for unending development; 3) tensions of dependence/independence or action/receptivity are always capable of being worked out in richer ways; and 4) the de-absolutizing of idols remains the constant religious vocation until death. Rather than being presented as an image of a plateau or a peak, this third stage, the stage of religious adulthood, embraces the image of a journey toward the center of oneself and of the universe.[60]

Moran is concerned that Fowler might be giving control of the word *religious* to the fixed forms and institutions we call religions. *Religion,* however, is to be distinguished from *religious.* "The individual's faith," states Moran, "is not a passive acquiring of creeds and practices but a means by which the tradition is re-created and transformed . . . one must clear the ground of atrophied religion so that a personal religious life can blossom. The next generation, of course, has to repeat the process: A tradition while being passed on needs to be continually renewed.[61] Finally, Moran advises:

> A scheme of religious development has to allow for alternate journeys. However, one cannot get rid of centuries of religious development by simply stepping out of them. Religious development does not proceed by wrenching out one idea and substituting another. Development means slowly becoming another person as the language of our community shapes and reshapes the whole of life . . . I do not see that the term *faith development* can carry the whole, even if one were to broaden the meaning of faith beyond mental structures to include beliefs. What can and should be studied is religious activity, including beliefs. Religious activities shift from one pattern to another in course of a person's life. These patterns are visible wholes that cannot be captured in exclusively psychological terms.[62]

For Moran, religious development is a life-long journey that begins at birth, or perhaps even earlier, and continues unto death.[63] Religious education is seminal as a guide within this journey. But it is religious maturity, not maturity in faith, that is the central concern of religious education. Moran's argument certainly can be persuasive. But where does religious education take place?

THE CONTEXT OF RELIGIOUS EDUCATION

Gabriel Moran claims that modern education needs the religious for its own good and even for its own meaning. The incorporation of a religious dimension into modern education would allow for a richer religious dimension in one's life. It could bring vitality to the discussion of all education, and it would characterize the aim of education as never ending. Thus, Moran suggests a model of education that has several well-defined forms where religious practices and language would be welcomed.[64]

A Model of Education: Educational Life Forms

Religious education is education. And its context is the arena of education, with its multiple life forms. In the first section of this chapter, Moran's model of education was sketched. This included the life forms of family, school, work, and leisure. These forms provide settings for religious education that, in both the past and present, have contributed to how people learn. Nearly everyone shares these forms. It is through the tension and the interplay of these forms that education emerges.[65]

The settings for these life forms are to be appropriate according to the needs of the age. This would require the teacher to be aware of the aims of religious education in relation to the age and personal characteristics of the learner. In addition, the physical as well as the social setting of where the teaching takes place is to be taken into consideration. We now turn to Moran's thoughts concerning the various settings for and of religious education.

Religious and educational formation usually occurs first within the family. This setting is the natural place for the first phase of religious education, amidst parents, grandparents, and siblings who serve as the child's first teachers. The family remains central in the nurturing and rearing of children. It should be noted that the family is not to be equated with the larger community but should be included in the community. According to Moran, both the family and the community need to be held in healthy tension with one another. The family, for its own good, needs other communal groupings such as the neighborhood or a religious congregation. For the good of the community, the family needs to be included in community discussions. Such an enterprise requires shaping and reshaping of the relationship between family and community. Education provides the means with which to do so.[66]

As the child's ability to understand begins to grow, the classroom of the school is an educational setting. The classroom is designed to promote knowledge through the person of the teacher, books, and computers that assist the processes of probing, questioning, and understanding. The classroom also provides the setting for religious education and for the understanding of religion as an academic subject.

The understanding of religion begins in childhood but should become the primary task of the high school classroom. Classrooms for teaching/learning religion should be available throughout adulthood as well.[67]

School also should be a place for young people to experience real work before they enter the job/working world. Such experience would help young persons appreciate genuine work for itself, not just as a job or the means for making money.

A religious education can assist one to make wise choices within a work setting as well. Examples of this might include recognizing that: 1) While supporting a family is important, one should also be concerned with worth-while work rather than the greatest salary possible; 2) While possessing entrepreneurial talents, the individual chooses to work in a collaborative way with a community or peers; and 3) Although skillfully trained, the individual embraces a reverence for living things and recognizes human limitations.[68]

In the latter part of life, leisure comes to the center as a significant educational form. Other than meaning "free time from work", Moran calls for a re-appropriation and a reinstitution of the classical meaning of the word, *leisure.* The term is to be associated with *contemplation* that would indicate an attitude of peace, wholeness and centeredness for all persons. Contemplation is to be preserved and embodied in the family setting, the school one attends and in the work one does. Looking for places and times of quiet in these settings cultivates a contemplative attitude.[69]

These life forms occur in various settings for a religious education. As a whole, the life forms of family (community), schooling (literate knowledge), job (work), and leisure (contemplative wisdom) provide a full and rich religious education for the individual from birth to death.

The work of Maria Harris applies these educational forms to a church setting. The church, she writes, provides a setting for the implementation of these foundational forms for religious education. Harris references the spawning of these forms in the second chapter of the Book of Acts (2:42, 44-47) where communion, prayer, care for the needy, the preached word, and teaching are basic forms for the church's curriculum. She suggests that from an ecclesial perspective, church curriculum is usually sequential, beginning with a gathered community *(koinonia)* for the main purpose to worship God through liturgical prayer *(leiturgia)* and to engage in works that serve justice *(diakonia).* It is only when the first three are in place do the curricular acts of preaching *(kerygma)* and gathering for instruction and catechesis *(didache)*— both of which are largely verbal—make sense.[70]

In summary, wherever religious education takes place, the process that occurs between the teacher and the learner is crucial. The act of teaching/learning therefore is pertinent to the process of religious education. If religious education is to be recognized, it needs to include a wider and deeper meaning of teaching other than providing explanations to children. For Mary Boys, the act of teaching is concerned with more than merely transmitting or telling information; teaching involves attention to the engagement of appropriate knowledge, ways of questioning, proper modes of providing responses and evaluation and "small acts of grace" that make human interaction humane.[71] In order to explore the act of teaching/learning, we now turn to the "how" of religious education, and to the methodologies that invoke the processes of teaching religion and teaching one to be religious.

EDUCATIONAL METHODOLOGY IN CONTEMPORARY RELIGIOUS EDUCATION

A method is an approach. It is a way of proceeding. Following the two main aims of religious education, its way of proceeding is multiple. Its varied processes, according to Gabriel Moran, can be captured with the verb "to teach."

The Meaning of Teaching

In an attempt to find a meaning for the verb "to teach" perhaps it would be appropriate first to discern what "to teach" is not.

First, teaching, while related to education, is not the whole of education. Teaching is an act that has a nature of its own. Second, teaching is not a process where one person exercises powerful control over others. If this latter statement is one that is recognized as the meaning of teaching, then "it is almost certain to corrupt the relation between teacher and student. This corruption is the reason for the ambivalence expressed about teaching . . . an ambivalence that ranges from mild suspicion to total opposition."[72] Third, Gabriel Moran suggests that teaching is not an act performed by only those who are professionally trained. It is an act performed by every human being.

In fleshing out the verb "to teach," Moran proposes an etymological starting point. *To teach,* he explains, "has always meant and still means 'to show', and by immediate extension, to show someone how to do something."[73] Moran's seminal work on teaching, *Showing How: The Act of Teaching,* is fundamental for probing the meaning of teaching and disclosing the various processes of religious education.

Showing How: Re-grounding the Verb "To Teach"

For Moran, the phrase "showing how" is most closely correlated with "learning how" rather than "knowing how." "Showing how", he writes, is accomplished through the continuity of teaching and learning:

> The rejection of the assumption that teaching and learning are separate things
> will lead to new questions about what teaching means and has meant for a thou-

sand years. I begin with the premise that learning always implies teaching. In fact, the only proof that teaching exists is the existence of learning. The way to avoid the equation of teaching and intention is to say that teaching is the showing how in the process of teaching-learning. Teaching is showing someone how to live and how to die. Someone learns these things because he or she has been taught.[74]

It is important then to realize who and what teaches. Moran points out that the universe that consists of living and nonliving things, has the ability to show someone how to do something. Included in these "things" would be: things of nature such as the ocean or animals; persons; books; and the individual whose experience allows her/himself to act as teacher. What is necessary to learn from these teachers, living and non-living, human and non-human, is the necessity of a dialectical relation that may provide an instructive element for understanding teach-learn in the world of living beings.[75]

If one is to agree with Gabriel Moran that various institutional settings support education, namely, the life forms of family, school, work, and leisure, then, one realizes that each institution presents a variety of teacher types. Such types would include: diverse family members, religious leaders/educators, mentors, the church community, and schoolteachers. In other words, the meaning of *teacher* includes but involves more than the image of the *schoolteacher*. Moran explains:

A teacher shows someone else how to do something. In the act of teaching, words are choreography for the body's movement. Good teachers have the know-how to break up a complex activity in ways that help the learner. Schoolteaching is a peculiar kind of teaching, a limit situation in which the words are mainly about words. Schoolteaching can therefore be the emptiest kind of teaching, although when the conditions are right it can be very powerful. A long-standing argument concerns whether anyone can teach if no one is learning. The answer to that question is: Yes, in the limit situation of schoolteaching. In more normal situations (e.g., teaching a child to ride a bicycle) the teaching and learning are so bodily related that the question can hardly arise, for teacher and learner have a sense of mutual success or mutual failure . . . teaching is the specifically human help that any person can give to another.[76]

With this inclusive meaning of teaching, Moran proceeds to name the various teaching forms, and in doing so illuminates the various processes or methods of religious education.

Teaching by Design: Non-Verbal Forms of Teaching

Humans teach by design. "The person who sets out to teach someone something," Moran notes, "inevitably attempts to impose some design. What the teacher discovers in this attempt is that every human design is a redesign. The best that a teacher can do is work with student and environment to improve the present design."[77] An alternative understanding of "to teach" is to find out what *is* teaching in a particular situation and then direct one's attention to redesigning these forces.

The "good" teacher, then, 1) will realize that, at times, it is the learner who becomes the teacher; 2) is a person who is not opposed to a learner's freedom; 3) builds a relation of trust; 4) relates the person's activity and the environment; 5) creates an environment that reduces the threat level; and 6) promotes dialogue. The ability to realize these situations points to the ability of the teacher to have a sense of the gap between the teacher's intention and the student's learning.[78]

Moran offers the metaphor of design and redesign for the potential learner; it is doing something; to teach is to change what is being done. The pattern is student acts, teacher studies design, teacher proposes redesign, student acts differently. Therefore, all teaching-learning is by doing.[79] This form of teaching could be applied to the re-design of family, work, and classrooms.

Teaching with an End in View: Verbal Forms of Teaching

Moran portrays a "family" of languages that are used in teaching. The languages are homiletic, therapeutic, and academic. Teaching with an end in view calls for a particular linguistic form. This family of languages arises from a community existence. Every community has a set of beliefs, and the languages are intended to persuade people to act on the basis of those beliefs.

The conviction that the end is known is embodied in the community's existence—the good to be attained by this group is evident. It is the teacher's task to link the past with this end in the future so that the energies of the present are unleashed. The great teacher knows how to touch persons so that they are moved to action. In a genuine community, the teacher seizes the moment to shape the words for their greatest effect, relying on a style that is in touch with memory, faithfulness, hopes, and conviction.[80]

Moran provides three examples of teaching and languages of teaching with an end in view. They are storytelling, lecturing, and preaching.

1) Storytelling encompasses oral and literary forms; it is a universal human trait. It has the power to shape the lives of people whether it is fact or fiction. Moran points out that today's stories may be absent of a trusted narrator, someone to tell the whole story and where it all leads. Yet the term "story" remains present and so needs other languages of teaching to complement and sometimes precede storytelling.[81]

2) Lecturing has a particular kind of instructive or didactic purpose. Lecturing is a highly ritualized act in which a person addresses a community; the end that the lecture has in view is some rational conception of humanity:

> For teaching by lecture, the speaker and the text need a ritualized setting. The listeners need to be capable of appreciating well-written prose delivered with a forceful style. The author needs to speak words that come from the depth of self. The aim of the lecture is to change, however imperceptibly, the listener's actions as a human being."[82]

3) Preaching is different from lecturing in that the latter is read and the former is the spoken word. Preaching is closely identified with the church that developed it into an art form. The text expresses the community's beliefs and its intention is to move people to do something about the injustices in the world. A test for a preacher is to stir the hearts of the community with its intimate language while not insulting or offending outsiders.[83] These teaching languages described by Moran are viable both inside and outside the church. They are indispensable in teaching people to be religious.

Teaching to Remove Obstacles: The Use of Therapeutic Language

Moran suggests that the use of language in teaching has therapeutic properties because such language has the ability to calm, soothe and heal. Therapy is a central need in human life and should be recognized as central to teaching. "What most people do need at certain moments of a day, a year, or a lifetime," Moran notes, "is the help of restorative language . . . The point of the conversation is not to reach any particular conclusion; it is to allow the force of life in the form of the will to reemerge in the context of ordinary life."[84] He illustrates this cluster of language with three paired terms with the explanation that the person teaching can be on either side of the pair, and the teacher and the learner can easily reverse positions. The healing occurs in the form of receiving and giving. The three pairs are welcome/thank, confess/forgive, mourn/comfort. These words put into action can be powerful and the use of them, in the teaching process, has the ability to remove obstacles that may inhibit the effect of healing and learning within a community. This teaching and language form is vital in the process of teaching to be religious.

Teaching the Conversation: The Use of Academic Language

Teaching is always a form of conversation; to be taught as a human is to enter the human conversation. This is a more specific type of teaching. Here one is concerned with speech about speech. It is about reaching understanding; it is about the meaning and questioning the texts; how to speak so that greater understanding is possible; it is about making the distinction between truth and meaning. Here is where the teacher choreographs, not a movement of body, but a movement of language.

Moran presents three forms for teaching the conversation. They are dramatic performance or a "play," dialectical discussion, and academic criticism.

1) Dramatic performances can have directly instructive purposes intending to convey a message. In a staged play, the teacher is not an individual but the interplay of actor with actor, actors with audience.[85]

2) Dialectical discussion can include philosophical thinking but also can embrace ordinary discussions that bend back the meaning of the terms in use. One could speak of debate or argument here, as long as it refers to a quest for meaning rather than a scoring of points.[86]

3) Academic criticism incorporates all the previous forms of language, giving it its potential. With this form of language, the student is the participant and the ultimate hope for a positive effect is to criticize or call into question part of the established world. Moran believes academic criticism has the potential to be among the most powerful of teaching languages. This teaching form, with its distinctive language, is indispensable for engaging the other side of religious education, namely, teaching religion as an academic subject.

In choreographing a movement of language and doing so with the appropriate language for a particular occasion of teaching, the teacher can arrange the environment for fruitful teaching/ learning. This is what it means to teach morally: do the right thing in the right setting.

This exploration of the meaning of teaching opens up for us the plurality of methods and processes appropriate for contemporary religious education.

Does a parish/church setting provide a sufficient and an efficient environment for such language forms to be instrumental in educating religiously? Does ecclesial life have room for academic language? Do religious institutions encourage fruitful teaching/learning? Or is their only main concern "teaching with an end in view", namely, initiation into a faith community? And what is the role of theology in the teaching/learning process? We turn now to this perennial question in religious education.

THE RELIGIOUS FOUNDATIONS OF
CONTEMPORARY RELIGIOUS EDUCATION

While theology has held a dominant place in the churches, the role of theology in the educational process has been a source of conflict and tension in the field of religious education.[87] Norma H. Thompson points out several questions related to this concern: 1) Does theology determine (or influence) decisions regarding the content of religious education? 2) How does theology affect methodology, objectives, curriculum, and administration of religious education? 3) Do the problems of communication prohibit or impede discussion of the issues in depth? 4) While it can be acknowledged that the various terms *religious education, Christian education, church education, Christian nurture, catechetics,* and *catechesis* relate to the educational task, is there an equally diverse set of meanings for theological terms such as *God, church, salvation, redemption, revelation* and *liberation?* 5) Does the educational process itself have a creative role to play in religious education that would reconstruct and reinterpret the basic concepts of a religion? What would be the result of such an interaction of theology and the educational process? 6) What is the impact of a growing pluralism in religion on the question of the role of theology? Is this issue problematic for all Christian and non-Christian religions? Is there a possible, adequate resolution of this issue for all?[88]

These questions call for clarity. However, before delving into these concerns, it is necessary to first provide some various viewpoints concerning the historical relationship between theology and religious education.

The Relationship between Theology and Religious Education

Mary C. Boys shares the view: to bring clarity to the field of religious education, it is necessary to acknowledge the different and necessary contributions that both theology and religious studies have made and continue to make to the field of religious education. However, Boys points out a problematic situation for religious educators: theologians have been "largely inclined to subsume religious education under the rubric of that chameleon division, practical theology."[89] In other words, an existing dichotomy between theology and religious education has generally determined them to be separate and unequal, with the former being "imperialistic" to the latter.[90]

Some contemporary religious theorists, such as Episcopalian Randolph Crump Miller and Roman Catholic educator Berard Marthaler perceive religious education as being placed within the context of (pastoral) theology. Miller, however, calls for both religious education and theology to be in dialogue with one another. Sara Little and John Westerhoff have similar sentiments.

Little perceives the role of theology in religious education as 1) providing content to be taught but not as a tool for indoctrination; 2) a point of reference for the interpretation and evaluation of practices, systems, and structures, thus being instrumental for communicating a way to be educated as well as simultaneously contributing to theological reformulations; and 3) an important discipline of religious education that should, however, take into consideration psychology and social sciences as educational decisions are being made.[91]

Westerhoff argues that religious education is more catechetical than theological. He suggests that theology should be related to the process of catechesis in ways that maintain the integrity and value of each.

Mary Boys calls for a reconsideration of the relationship of theology and religious education. In doing so, she suggests particular role(s) for theology in its relationship with religious education. She proposes 1) theology is significant for religious education since it a) offers a means of constructing analytical categories to examine past and present movements, events, theorists and programs; b) gives some methodologies useful for constructing one's own world view; c) provides significant knowledge; 2) theology does not suffice for religious education. Therefore, religious education is not to be understood primarily as a subdivision of practical theology since theology is only one way of understanding religion; theology is to be a part of religious education but is not to control it; 3) since theology is concerned with questions of both meaning and truth, it is to serve as a model for religious educators; It is the theological dimension that distinguishes the religious educator from the general educator. Boys advises that religious education needs to maintain its distinct identity. She acknowledges that such an endeavor needs to be supported by an extended examination of the meaning of education.[92] Such an examination is needed to clarify what methodologies Boys believes theology can provide.

James Michael Lee argues that religion and theology are distinct. The language of the former is fundamentally personal, while the language of the latter is basically propositional. Thus, Lee perceives religious instruction (his word) and theology as having distinct natures, operating on different levels of reality. Lee compares these distinctions: 1) religion is a basic way of living; theology is primarily a cognitive affair; 2) religion is a way of life; theology is a theory about this way of life; 3) religion exists primarily and directly to enable individuals to live enriched God-filled lives; theology exists primarily and directly to provide cognitive information on God and God's revelatory activities that is also helpful for living an enriched religious life; 4) religion is a way of life, and therefore makes lifestyle and often confessional demands upon the learner when it is facilitated; theology is a cognitive science, and therefore makes no lifestyle or confessional demands upon the learner when it is facilitated. Based on these distinctions,

Lee concludes, "Christian living and thought concerning God are not the same thing. Though religion and theology may intersect each other under certain circumstances, nonetheless they are basically different modes of human activity. Theology is dependent upon religion but is not identical to religion."[93]

These thoughts are the basis for Lee's criticism about some of the existing distinctions and misunderstandings that dilute religious instruction as a delivery system for theology and as a translator of theoretical understandings into existential situations.[94]

Concerning the relationship of theology and religious education, Gabriel Moran believes that while theology can supply part of the content of religious education, it cannot provide all of the content. "Theology," he writes, "has nothing to offer concerning the method, structure, and institutional form of religious education."[95] Theology, historically, has been an obstacle to the development to the field of religious education. It ought, Moran postulates, to become a modest contributor to the enterprise. We turn now to explore in greater detail Moran's perspective.

A Paradox in the Meanings of Religion and the Religious

A contributing factor to perceiving theology as an obstacle to religious education, according to Moran, is the existence of a paradox between *religion* and the *religious*. This paradox (that has been present throughout the twentieth century) assumes that existing religions eliminate the possibility of being religious. Moran explains the paradox in the following two statements: 1) the evidence is that to be Christian, Jewish, Muslim, one should be committed to it as the truth, the life, the path. Each demands not an academic curiosity but a wholehearted commitment of oneself, not a general interest but an intense devotion; and 2) the existence of a diversity of these "one ways" seems to undercut the possibility that Christian, Jewish, Muslim, or any other group can maintain its traditional position while accepting the "many ways" that modern education readily acknowledges.[96]

Modern science and religions to this day contribute to this paradox. The former, while having produced some valuable information and understanding, has not been able to transform religions by its rationalist approach. The latter finds Christian, Jewish, or Muslim leaders speaking the peculiar inner language of their own traditions.

These approaches to the religious life, for Moran, cannot provide an adequate basis for a religious education. If religious education is to develop, a comprehensive and systematic approach to the religious is needed.

Kieran Scott contributes to this argument by acknowledging that if religious education is to emerge as an academically respectable field and profession in its own right, it needs to be more than a subdivision of theology or confined to its framework. Scott offers two reasons for his viewpoint: 1) a vast treasure of religious material and experience lies beyond the realm of theology; so opportunities for more religious content that is beyond the theological should be offered in the educational curriculum; and 2) The theological enterprise needs a broad ecumenical, educational, and developmental framework in the contemporary religious context. Religious educators would then be able to explore their own tradition and challenge its claims in relation to other traditions thus evoking a free response. They also need an open and pluralistic context to "explore with tolerance the vital religious issues confronting them in the modern world."[97]

Religious education must insist upon thinking through the way of being religious in a context of education. Theology cannot perform that function. "That entails," Gabriel Moran states, "thinking through the meaning of one's own religious life in relation to both those who share that life and those who do not."[98] This process recognizes the need for religious education and a language that can mediate these divisions. Theology cannot mediate these divisions. It is already on one side of the divide. An alternative religious language, not burdened with theological assumptions, is what is required in these circumstances.

Theology as Modest Contributor

For Moran, who speaks from his own Christian/Catholic theological experience, the teaching and study of theology differs from the teaching and study of religion. Theology can supply part of the content for religious education. It, however, is too closely associated with the inner language of a particular religion. In the educational context of religious education, theological content would be subject to criticism. How do religions fare with such critique? Do religions possess the ability to be open to such critique? Can such openness to an educational process exist when theology is seen as the major supplier of content in educational endeavors? Does the freedom to ask non-theological questions exist in a religious educational setting? Is such action encouraged or discouraged in the educational settings of religious institutions?

Perhaps critical here is theology's ability to be separated from its historical association with the question of *orthodoxy*. Moran doubts if such a notion is possible since 1) the limitation of orthodoxy guarantees that one is dealing with more than a passing fad; and 2) theology avoids being merely academic because it lays claim to divine truth.[99] He also points out: while some of the elaborate systems of theology can provide some of the content for religious education, they cannot claim to own the field of religious education and/or the control of it.[100]

Theology has an important but modest role within the developing field of religious education. Theology is a scientific discipline with distinctive Christian origins and assumptions. While attempts have been made to expand the meaning of the term, some fundamental challenges inhibit this effort.

If theology is to be fully recognized within a truly religious educational setting, it needs to step beyond the inner language of religious traditions before it can claim to cover the entire ground for the systematic study of the religious life. Moran offers the following criteria for such a claim: 1) theology can be as much a non-Christian word as a Christian word; 2) theology can describe ways of speaking and writing that are presentational as well as discursive, which means that poetry or biography are not just lesser forms of a properly doctrinal theology; and 3) that theology is not under the direct rule or subtle control of orthodoxy.[101] This is not likely to happen.

On the other hand, what is needed today is a bridge between religions and between religious language and non-religious speech. Core to this suggestion are the religious need of our times and an educational approach to religion. The religious, rather than the theological, is the foundation of contemporary religious education. Religious questions and concerns need to be worked out today in a religious context, i.e. an inter-religious setting. The religious is wider in scope and richer in meaning than one of its components, namely, the theological. And, within this diverse religious world, religious education is to be instrumental in challenging and transforming the ways of religious traditions.

We are compelled, however, to ask: Are these traditions open to this field of religious education that might provide rich, meaningful and life-giving contributions to the process of educating religiously in our contemporary world? Is the ecclesial world of catechesis open to this challenge?

SUMMARY

In this chapter, we have explored the theoretical origins, contemporary meaning, and the contemporary framework of religious education. This has been accomplished through the study of a re-conceptualized vision of religious education's: 1) meaning and identity; 2) meaning of religious

maturity; 3) context; 4) educational methodologies; and 5) religious foundations. The "what," "where," "who," "when," "how," and "why" of religious
education have been explored in order to reveal the second partner for the
conversation.

While this re-conceptualized religious education invokes critical questioning, the concern here is whether this form of religious education can
be a partner with catechesis in the process of religiously educating Roman
Catholics. This partnership seems absent in the recent *National Directory
of Catechesis.* However, the central question is: Can both partners contribute to a richer experience? What would or could be the benefit of such a
partnership? Does each enterprise view the other as a partner or as a threat?
What are the obstacles that might prevent a possible relationship? Would
both partners be better with or without one another? Or do they have irreconcilable differences?

These questions can only be addressed if both contemporary catechesis
and religious education are brought into conversation with one other. This,
and the implications of such a conversation, will be the task of the last
chapter.

NOTES

1. John Westerhoff, *Who Are We? The Quest For a Religious Education* (Birmingham: Religious Education Press, 1978), 3.

2. *The Aims of Religious Education,* The Proceedings of the Third Annual Convention of the Religious Education Association, Boston (Chicago: Religious Education Association, 1905) in Kenneth R. Barker, *Religious Education, Catechesis, and
Freedom* (Birmingham: Religious Education Publishing, 1981), 27.

3. Westerhoff, *Who Are We? The Quest For a Religious Education,* 13.

4. Mary C. Boys, *Educating in Faith: Maps and Visions* (Lima, OH: Academic
Renewal Press, 1989), 126.

5. The working meaning of *religious education* throughout the study is that es-
poused by Gabriel Moran, Maria Harris, Kieran Scott, and the later works of Mary
Boys. No monolithic meaning of *religious education* exists today. Alternate viewpoints exist. Some conceptualize *religious education* as a form of pastoral theology
(Thomas Groome, Berard Marthaler). Others see *religious education* as a canopy term
in which Christianity, Jewish and Islam education can function as a subset (Westerhoff). But the operational meaning in this study is particularly that of the work of
Gabriel Moran.

6. Gabriel Moran, "The Intersection of Religion and Education" *Religious Education,* 69 no. 5 (1974): 532.

7. Moran, "The Intersection of Religion and Education," 540-41.

8. Moran, "The Intersection of Religion and Education," 538-40.

9. Gabriel Moran, "Two Languages of Religious Education" *The Living Light* 14 no. (1977): 8.

10. Moran, "Two Languages of Religious Education," 10.

11. Moran, "Two Languages of Religious Education," 10.

12. Moran, "Two Languages of Religious Education," 11.

13. Moran, "Two Languages of Religious Education," 11.

14. Moran, "Two Languages of Religious Education," 11.

15. Moran, "Two Languages of Religious Education," 52.

16. Moran, "Two Languages of Religious Education," 14.

17. Moran, "Two Languages of Religious Education," 14-15.

18. Gabriel Moran, *Religious Education As A Second Language* (Birmingham: Religious Education Press, 1989), 217.

19. Moran, *Religious Education As A Second Language*, 87.

20. Finola Cunnane, "Issues of Identity in Religious Education" in *Critical Issues in Religious Education*, ed. Oliver Brennan, 37 (Dublin: Veritas, 2005).

21. Moran, *Religious Education As A Second Language*, 229-30.

22. Moran, *Religious Education As A Second Language*, 232.

23. Moran, *Religious Education As A Second Language*.232.

24. Moran, *Religious Education As A Second Language*, 234.

25. Maria Harris and Gabriel Moran, *Reshaping Religious Education* (Louisville: Westminster, John Knox Press, 1998), 18.

26. Moran, *Religious Education as a Second Language*, 239.

27. Moran, *Religious Education as a Second Language*, 241.

28. Gabriel Moran, "Understanding Religion and Being Religious," *Pace* 21, (1992): 249.

29. Gabriel Moran, "Religious Education After Vatican II," Open Catholicism: The Tradition At Its Best ed. David Efroymson and John Raines 157 (Collegeville: The Liturgical Press, 1997).

30. Moran in *Reshaping Religious Education*, 43.

31. Kieran Scott, "Three Traditions of Religious Education," Religious Education, 79 no. 6 (1984): 336.

32. Scott, "Three Traditions of Religious Education," 337.

33. See the *National Directory for Catechesis*, no. 48.

34. See Berard Marthaler, "Socialization as a Model for Catechetics" *Sourcebook for Modern Catechetics Volume 2*, ed. Michael Warren 136 (Winona: Saint Mary's Press, 1997).

35. Felicity B. Kelcourse. "Theories of Human Development" in *Human Development and Faith: Life-Cycle Stages of Body, Mind, and Soul*, ed. Felicity B. Kelcourse, 45 (St Louis: Chalice Press, 2004).

36. James W. Fowler, *Stages of Faith: The Psychology of Human Development and the Quest For Meaning* (San Francisco: Harper, 1981), 14-15.

37. Fowler, *Stages of Faith: The Psychology of Human Development and the Quest For Meaning*, 114.

38. Fowler, *Stages of Faith: The Psychology of Human Development and the Quest For Meaning*, 49.

39. Fowler, *Stages of Faith: The Psychology of Human Development and the Quest For Meaning*, 49.

40. Fowler, *Stages of Faith: The Psychology of Human Development and the Quest For Meaning*, 49.

41. Fowler, *Stages of Faith: The Psychology of Human Development and the Quest For Meaning*, 121.

42. Fowler, *Stages of Faith: The Psychology of Human Development and the Quest For Meaning*, 133-34.

43. Fowler, *Stages of Faith: The Psychology of Human Development and the Quest For Meaning*, 149-50.

44. Fowler, *Stages of Faith: The Psychology of Human Development and the Quest For Meaning*, 172-73.

45. Fowler, *Stages of Faith: The Psychology of Human Development and the Quest For Meaning*, 183.

46. Fowler, *Stages of Faith: The Psychology of Human Development and the Quest For Meaning*, 183.

47. Fowler, *Stages of Faith: The Psychology of Human Development and the Quest For Meaning*, 199.

48. Kelcourse, "Theories of Human Development," 47.

49. Gabriel Moran, *Religious Education Development: Images for the Future* (Minneapolis: Winston Press, 1983), 107.

50. Moran, *Religious Education Development: Images for the Future*, 107-108.

51. Moran, *Religious Education Development: Images for the Future*, 122.

52. Moran, *Religious Education Development: Images for the Future*, 125.

53. Moran, *Religious Education Development: Images for the Future*, 18.

54. Moran, *Religious Education Development: Images for the Future*, 114.

55. Moran, *Religious Education Development: Images for the Future*, 110.

56. Moran, *Religious Education Development: Images for the Future*, 113.

57. Moran, *Religious Education Development: Images for the Future*, 133.

58. Moran, *Religious Education Development: Images for the Future*, 153-54.

59. Moran, *Religious Education Development: Images for the Future*, 146-56.

60. Moran, *Religious Education Development: Images for the Future*, 132.

61. Moran, *Religious Education Development: Images for the Future*, 134.

62. Moran, *Religious Education Development: Images for the Future*, 140-43.

63. See Moran, "Development and Death" in *Reshaping Religious Education*, Chapter 6.

64. Gabriel Moran, Interplay: A Theory of Religion and Education (Winona: St. Mary's Press, 1981) 46.

65. Moran, Interplay: *A Theory of Religion and Education*, 44-45.

66. Moran, *Reshaping Religious Education*, 39-42.

67. Moran, *Reshaping Religious Education*, 41-42.

68. Moran, *Reshaping Religious Education*, 204.

69. See Chapter 6, "Work and Leisure Within Religious Education" in Moran's Interplay, 79-90.

70. Harris, *Reshaping Religious Education*, 20-21.

71. Mary Boys refers here to the work of Kenneth Elbe, *The Craft of Teaching.* (San Francisco: Jossey-Bass, 1976) in "Teaching: The Heart of Religious Education," *Religious Education Journal*, 79:2 (Spring, 1984), 264.

72. Moran in *Religious Education as a Second Language*, 64.

73. Gabriel Moran, *Showing How: The Act of Teaching* (Valley Forge: Trinity Press International, 1997), 37.

74. Moran, *Showing How: The Act of Teaching*, 41.

75. Moran, *Showing How: The Act of Teaching*, 46-47.

76. Moran, *Religious Education Development*, 161-62.

77. Moran, *Showing How: The Act of Teaching*, 59.

78. Moran, *Showing How: The Act of Teaching*, 60-67, 74.

79. Moran, *Showing How: The Act of Teaching*, 71.

80. Moran, *Showing How: The Act of Teaching*, 86-87.

81. Moran, *Showing How: The Act of Teaching*, 94.

82. Moran, *Showing How: The Act of Teaching*, 96.

83. Moran, *Showing How: The Act of Teaching*, 98-100.

84. Moran, *Showing How: The Act of Teaching*, 106-7.

85. Moran, *Showing How: The Act of Teaching*, 130-32.

86. Moran, *Showing How: The Act of Teaching*, 132-33.

87. Norma H. Thompson, "The Role of Theology in Religious Education: An Introduction" *Religious Education and Theology* ed. Norma H. Thompson, 2 (Birmingham: Religious Education Press, 1982).

88. Thompson, "The Role of Theology in Religious Education: An Introduction," 14.

89. Mary C. Boys, "The Role of Theology in Religious Education" in *Horizons*, 11:1 (1984): 61.

90. Boys, "The Role of Theology in Religious Education," 62.

91. Boys, "The Role of Theology in Religious Education," 68.

92. Boys, "The Role of Theology in Religious Education," 80-85.

93. James Michael Lee. "The Authentic Source of Religious Instruction" *Religious Education and Theology* ed. Norma H. Thompson, 109-10 (Birmingham: Religious Education Press, 1982).

94. Lee, "The Authentic Source of Religious Instruction," 70-71.

95. Gabriel Moran, "From Obstacle to Modest Contributor: Theology in Religious Education" *Religious Education and Theology* ed. Norma H. Thompson, 42 (Birmingham: Religious Education Press, 1982).

96. Moran, "From Obstacle to Modest Contributor," 50.

97. Scott, "Three Traditions of Religious Education," 332.

98. Moran, "From Obstacle to Modest Contributor," 52.

99. Moran, "From Obstacle to Modest Contributor," 55.

100. Moran, "From Obstacle to Modest Contributor," 56.

101. Moran, "From Obstacle to Modest Contributor," 59.

Chapter Five

Searching for and Initiating a Conversation

INTRODUCTION

While the *National Directory for Catechesis* remains central to the purpose of this book, the directory may evoke an intuitive uneasiness. Such a reaction might be indicative of tension that exists between the fields of catechesis and religious education. This tension might be exacerbated by a sense that something is lacking in the catechetical enterprise as it is presented in the Directory. What appears to be absent from the Directory is the recognition and presence of the field of religious education.

As noted in the introduction of this book, the terms *catechesis* and *religious education* have, at times, been used interchangeably in the Roman Catholic documents. Although the *National Directory for Catechesis* utilizes the term *catechesis* consistently throughout the document, it does refer to the term *religious education* at various points.[1] However, the explorations of both catechesis (as seen through the lens of the *NDC*) and the field of contemporary religious education in the previous chapters suggest the different and distinct natures of the two fields and the tension that exists between them. This book seeks to raise the question whether this tension is conflictual or creative. Would it be beneficial for the catechetical enterprise of the Catholic Church to partner with religious education? Would partnering with religious education foster a richer catechetical process that would be of benefit to the church in its mission and ministry?

The historical studies of the roots of both fields in Chapters 1 and 2 illustrate the distinct ancient history of catechesis, the distinct modern history of religious education, and the overlapping of their parallel developments and their conceptual differences in the second half of the twentieth century. Chapter 3 provides a study of the distinctive nature of catechesis, captured in the *National Directory for Catechesis*, a document written by and for the church.

The distinguishing characteristics of contemporary religious education were presented in Chapter 4.

It is the task now is to 1) address the absence of religious education in the *National Directory for Catechesis;* 2) determine the possible contributions a partnership with religious education could offer the field of catechesis; and 3) recognize what catechesis can contribute to the field of religious education. In order to meet this endeavor, the two practices of catechesis and religious education will be placed in a dialectical conversation.

The five themes that prevailed in Chapters 3 and 4 will include a particular category that has not been fully recognized before in this work, yet captures the essence of each theme. This process will set up the conversation in the following manner: 1) The meanings of catechesis and religious education will be broadened by acknowledging the specificity of their respective identities; 2) Conversion in catechesis and religious education will be presented as an essential component of maturity in faith/religious maturity; 3) The professions that are pertinent to the context of catechesis and religious education will be addressed; 4) The indispensable role of teaching within the framework of catechetical/educational methodologies will be recognized; and 5) The inclusion of religious pluralism will be considered in the theological/religious foundations of catechesis and religious education. The cornerstone for the conversation is provided by both the thematic content and tripartite purpose of the NDC; specifically: 1) to provide those fundamental theological and pastoral principals drawn from the Church's magisterium and to apply them to the pastoral activity of catechesis; 2) to offer guidelines for the application of those fundamental theological and pastoral principles in this country in order to promote a renewal of catechesis; and 3) to set forth the nature, purpose, object, tasks, basic content, and various methodologies of catechesis.[2] In addition, the practical and pastoral implications of the dialogue will be suggested.

Hopefully such an endeavor would contribute to the resolution of tension that exists between the fields of catechesis and religious education. The positive results of this conversation could result in a partnership of both fields that would enrich the educational processes of catechesis and the life of the church.

THE IDENTITIES OF CATECHESIS
AND RELIGIOUS EDUCATION

The meaning(s) of catechesis and religious education were studied in Chapters 3 and 4. While the identities of both were alluded to at that time, a deeper exploration of the identity of catechesis and religious education is necessary. Without such an exploration, the meaning of catechesis and religious education would remain wanting.

Identity and Language

Identity can be described as the sense of who we are and how we live. Identity causes one to live humanly; without it one would feel lost. Social scientists claim that identity holds together a continuous sense of being human as a person or as a community. Identity emerges as one absorbs the worldview, value system, and sense of person reflected in one's family of origin, culture, and society. Instrumental in this process are the symbols that are encountered and internalized.[3] In this regard, it is necessary to be attentive to the language of a people, of a community, since language provides concreteness, clarity, and practicality to identity. Gabriel Moran notes: " . . . the political and educational life of human beings throughout the centuries can be traced in the movement of language."[4]

The Languages of the National Directory for Catechesis and Religious Education

Religion has been described as a language; a cultural linguistic system that functions like a language or a culture. It dwells in the culture that has inherited it. It is spoken by and instrumental in the formation of a people. In other words, language provides a way of giving one a particular worldview, an outlook on life, expectations, and values.[5] Catechesis and religious education are such languages. Each offers its own language of education.

The *National Directory for Catechesis* provides us with the most contemporary language of catechesis. This is the internal language of the Roman Catholic Church. It is specific. Kieran Scott states: "This warm intimate, caressing language nurtures Catholic becoming and belonging. It fosters religious identity and cultivates convictional knowing and practice. Church ministers (catechists, homilists, liturgists) have a right and duty to preserve this internal language."[6] In preserving this language, the Catholic tradition is acquired, transmitted, rooted, and identified with a body of people and shaped into the character and meaning system of its communal life. Scott names this enterprise the *tribal phase* or the *inner border model* of religious education.[7]

Conceptually, this model adheres to its own tradition, one that processes enculturation, nurture, evangelization, and conversion. While the *National Directory for Catechesis* claims to position catechesis in a context of ecumenical and inter-religious dialogue,[8] it is mainly concerned with internal issues.

One of the functions of the directory is to apply the Roman Catholic Church's fundamental theological and pastoral principles drawn from the Church's magisterium to the pastoral activity of catechesis. This internal language is what Walter Bruggemann would describe as *conversation behind the wall;* a language concerned with the ordinary life of a people including the most intimate and sacred dealings in the community.[9] This language constitutes catechesis' role in affirming a religious tradition, fostering a denominational identity, and nurturing religious development. However, catechesis offers only one specific language. Therefore does the *National Directory for Catechesis* provide an adequate comprehensive context for meaningful dialogues in the contemporary world? Can the directory be instrumental in a public conversation with other religious traditions that exist in the United States? Is its language conducive to or limiting to such discussion?

Religious education, on the other hand, provides a second language in this context. It has the characteristics of a language that people learn after they have learned their native language. It has the ability to be public in nature. It can participate in conversation *at the wall.* Therefore, religious education is external, social, and visible. In contrast to catechesis, it cannot be confined to the private. It emerges with the movement of comparison between religious languages and then attempts to bring into conversation many religious languages. Gabriel Moran hypothesizes that the development and spread of the language of religious education is important to tolerance, understanding, and peace in the world.[10] Thus, in the same vein, Moran states:

> A religious education cannot abandon traditional religious language on the basis that it conflicts with what the modern world says is true. But equally important, religious education cannot be a settling for one's religious dialect without asking how it interacts with the modern world.[11]

By its nature, the language of religious education can be comfortable with both the religious and the secular. A re-conceptualized religious education, that was explored in Chapter 4, transcends the local ecclesial community. Scott would consider this form of religious education to be a *border crossing model.*[12]

For this model, education is the overall frame of reference and the arena for dealing with the critical religious issues and concerns of life. "It is the setting," states Scott, "in which diverse religious traditions (Catholic, Protestant, Jew, etc.) can converse on educational matters. Religion and education intersect in this interactive framework of critical appreciative intelligence."[13] A public language of religious education is needed for discourse in the public square.

Implications of the Conversation

By exposing the identities of catechesis and contemporary religious education, it can be acknowledged that the *NDC* embraces the inner border model of religious education. It appears to ignore a relationship with the larger world of education. Its language does not include an educational framework.

Set in a framework of church ministry, catechesis brings to the conversation an emphasis on and devotion to the traditional, ritual, sacramental, contemplative, and life-long development of its people. Kieran Scott states: "At its best, catechesis affirms rootedness in one's own religious tradition, fosters denominational identity and nurtures religious development."[14] These are positive characteristics. However, the catechetical language of the *NDC* promotes a turn toward the inner world of itself. It is in need of a complimentary language that would gather the Catholic Church's educational efforts and establish a bridge with other religious and educational agencies beyond it. The language of religious education would provide a framework where Catholic educational endeavors could encounter the endeavors of other religious traditions in the public square. This linguistic framework would prod catechesis from its own linguistic world and into a world of public speech, a world that is inclusive of all.

Education cultivates identity. Dependant on the stories or history of a people, education provides the insight into how a people were formed and what activities and institutions played a role in their formation and identity.[15] While embracing its own identity, the Catholic catechetical tradition cannot afford to ignore religious education. It appears that the *National Directory* has done just that; it has embraced its own internal identity, has remained loyal to its own language, and has ignored the language of religious education. People working in contemporary church ministry, in a word, need to become bi-lingual.

MATURITY IN FAITH AND RELIGIOUS MATURITY VIEWED THROUGH THE LENS OF CONVERSION

Pertinent in the development of one's maturity in faith (in catechetical terms, per the *NDC*) or religious maturity (in religious educational terms, per Moran), conversion is a pivotal ingredient for a richer religious and human experience. The meanings of *maturity in faith* and *religious maturity* include the experience of conversion. A description of *maturity in faith* is offered by the *NDC* as: "the faith of the disciple who has been saved by Christ's redemptive love and who is being continually converted to him."[16] Contemporary religious education acknowledges the possibility of three conversions as one passes through the stages of religious development, on the journey toward religious maturity.[17] Both catechesis and contemporary religious education, however, bring their particular vision of conversion to the conversation table. We begin with the meaning and essence of conversion in the *National Directory for Catechesis.*

Conversion in the *National Directory for Catechesis*

In Chapter 3, evangelization emerged as an important and necessary component in the catechetical enterprise. The *National Directory for Catechesis* reminds us that the *new evangelization* is "aimed at personal transformation through the development of a personal relationship with God, participation in sacramental worship, the development of a mature ethical and social conscience, ongoing catechesis, and a deepening integration of faith into all areas of life."[18] To bring about faith and conversion to Christ is the purpose of evangelization. In utilizing methods that help to bring about conversion, catechesis contributes to this process.

The *NDC* asserts that conversion to Christ is needed because human experience is affected by the fallen state of human nature and is in need of redemption in Jesus Christ. The *NDC* also reminds us that the human experience can be enlightened by Christ as well, thus generating an intimate, personal connection with Christ and the Christian message.[19]

Engendered by the Holy Spirit, this *metanoia* arises deep within one's being, where one faces the important questions of human life. This occurrence is manifested by a profound change of mind and heart, a transformation in the life of the individual.

Conversion to Jesus Christ is the epitome of Christianity, where one accepts a personal relationship with him and a willingness to conform one's life to his way. This personal decision is considered necessary for Christian discipleship. Such a decision also unites the Christian to the community of disciples, the church. The *NDC* explains:

> The process of conversion involves understanding who Christ is in order to change and follow him more closely. Conversion begins with an openness to the initial proclamation of the Gospel and a sincere desire to listen for resonance within. This search arouses in those coming to Christ a desire to know him more personally and to know more about him. This knowledge of the person, message, and mission of Christ enables the believer to "make it into a living, explicit and fruitful confession of faith."[20]

Conversion to Christ is necessary and continual, if one is to attain maturity in faith in the Roman Catholic tradition. Therefore, an attitude of conversion is to be nurtured in the believer. While this action is recognized as an aim for adult catechesis, the *NDC* does remark that children, engaged in the initiation process, are "capable of a conversion appropriate to their age."[21] Therefore, conversion to Christ is possible in varying degrees during the various stages throughout one's lifetime. Those responsible for catechesis are to be alert to this possibility. The *NDC* affirms: "Conversion to Christ is a lifelong process that should be accompanied at every stage by a vital catechesis that leads Christians on their journey towards holiness."[22] Does this mean that catechesis nurtures the individual *toward* holiness rather than *in* holiness? Is catechesis more focused on the "end product" of conversion rather than on the developmental process?

Conversion: Foundational to Religious Education

While conversion is foundational to Christianity, Mary Boys hypothesizes that conversion also is foundational to religious education. In other words, conversion plays a critical role in shaping educational practice.[23] Boys offers two points to support her argument:

1) While psychological studies can provide significant data about conversion, they neglect the *religious* aspect. Science cannot account for the transcendent in the conversion experience. Therefore, religious education forces the topic of conversion to include what theologically is referred to as *grace,* that which leads to the mystery of God's initiative and involvement in human life. As a result, the religious educator needs to realize the existence of a person's freedom before God.
2) Education is a summons to conversion, Boys also notes. At its best, education draws the individual outside of her/himself so that she/he might enter into lives, cultures, and perspectives that are different to one's own. Since God's ways are not easily discerned, education can provide the means to turn away from the sinfulness of ignorance and to counter the sense that one's self is the only reality.[24]

While the *NDC* alludes to varied usages of conversion, Boys specifically pinpoints and names three that have their own manifestations in our contemporary world. These are 1) entry into the Catholic Church—the result of a search of the truth that leads to an ecclesial commitment; 2) being *born again*—a classical meaning of conversion, to be *reborn again* is to move from the dark into the light accompanied by an awareness of an overwhelming need for rebirth in God's mercy; and 3) the quest for personal identity—by placing the self in the universe, one constructs a personal identity in accordance with a broader perspective. In doing so, self-knowledge is gained. The conflictual and lifelong process of becoming oneself is accompanied by the search for an adequate system of beliefs and values and the need to be purified and revivified. Seeing conversion in this light is to recognize that it is interwoven with one's entire life cycle, meaning that one grows religiously as well as in other dimensions of one's life.

For explanatory reasons, Boys refers to theologian Bernard Lonergan's reflective work on conversion. Lonergan understood conversion to lie at the center of religious experience. Without conversion, religion would be reduced to legalism, sentimentality or activism.[25]

Mary Boys also presents Lonergan's *three inter-related dimensions of conversion*. These dimensions are: 1) religious conversion—rooted in the powerful human longing for the transcendent, this dimension of conversion is a falling in love, a reverence for the Holy that transcends denominational affiliation; 2) moral conversion—making choices and decisions on the basis of values rather than on the basis of satisfaction, perhaps even paying a personal price for exacting a moral decision; and 3) intellectual conversion—turning away from the idolatry of easy answers and certitude and refusing to live in a secluded universe. Intellectual conversion brings a life-giving depth and breadth to religious and moral conversion; it allows one to believe in a God who is not threatened by one's doubts and questions.[26]

Education, Boys suggests, serves as a reminder that reality transcends the narrowness of our own experiences and feelings and remains a catalyst for conversion. Thus, she recommends that religious educators pay attention to the following: 1) maintain a balance of "readiness for learning" with an awareness of the educator's "readiness for teaching"; 2) make a lifelong commitment to learning; 3) expand one's images of God and of God's kingdom; 3) manifest a profound respect for the mystery of human development and for the time and pain it entails; and 4) see intellectual conversion as always in relation to religious and moral conversion since conversion on every level, the religious, moral and intellectual, is needed in order to carry out the Gospel message. In brief, religious education would stagnate without conversion.[27]

Conversion and Contemporary Religious Education

While Mary Boys maintains that conversion and religious education need one another for the vitality of each, Gabriel Moran advocates that religious development is required for the purpose of conversion. He proposes that the religious meaning of conversion can be made more intelligible if it is placed within a developmental framework. Continual conversion occurs because development provides continued growth or progress.[28]

Moran notes how developmental conversion bids individual progression, not toward an endpoint, but toward a greater integrity of life. He explains: "If forward movement is also a circling back, if outward movement is also an interior deepening, then the movement is not imagined as progress toward an object at the end."[29]

Moran acknowledges that there needs to be an unfolding of a development that "calls for a constant educational reshaping that deepens the sense of personal awareness and challenges the individual with the wisdom of the past . . . Without a *conversionary* development, the idea of development self-destructs either by smuggling in idols or by exhausting itself in unlimited growth."[30] Conversionary development is essential during the critical moments of one's life experience. Life crises cause a person to constantly circle back on his or her past for a context of interpretation. These crises can spawn conflicts between personal experience and the teachings of a religious tradition. The individual might struggle to discover whether the tradition any longer shapes her/his life. A thoughtful, reverence-full experience may allow the individual to feel justified in appealing beyond a particular teaching to the voice of the Holy Spirit within, to a future reform, or to a lost element of the tradition's past. Necessary for conversional development and religious maturity are common sense, modesty, and trust in experience and learning from God.[31]

Implications of the Conversation

Catechesis perceives a continual conversion to Christ that ensues throughout one's lifetime. This inner, deeper, conversional experience in and to Jesus Christ and the Church is vital for maturity in faith. The goal of this process is the attainment of holiness. It is the hope of the Catholic Church that all Christians " . . . in any state or walk of life are called to the fullness of Christian life and to the perfection of love, and by this holiness a more human manner of life is fostered also in earthly society."[32] This Catholic traditional view that catechesis brings to the conversation is to be preserved and recognized for its intent. As admirable as holiness and the Catholic perception and recognition of conversion might be, there can be more. This view is limiting in that it is placed *within the ecclesial wall*. It seems to be lacking an adequate, outward developmental quality. While the *Rite of Christian Initiation of Adults* embraces a developmental perspective that could enrich the whole of catechesis, it needs, in the words of Kieran Scott, "linkage to a variety of educational processes . . . Education with its multiple forms and diverse processes may be a friendly complement."[33]

Religious education, like catechesis, acknowledges that conversion is a lifelong process. Because of its developmental nature, a religious education educates one *in* conversion, not so much *toward* conversion. This process fosters *understanding* within the head, heart, and hands of the individual.

Catholic tradition offers an inner, deeper, conversional experience. Contemporary religious education views conversion as a spiraling outward. In other words, conversion, in this sense, draws the individual outside of her/himself so that she/he might enter into lives, cultures, religions, and perspectives that are different than one's own; it has the ability to help one be transformed in other areas of life in addition to the ecclesial. Such a perspective nourishes the wholeness of the person in her/his relations to other religious and non-religious aspects of life.

While catechesis and religious education have different views concerning the framework of conversion, what they have in common is the recognition of the need for a lifelong turning to God. Catechesis offers conversion as instrumental for the sake of *holiness*. Religious education offers a vision of conversion that helps the individual to develop into *wholeness* with all reality. The partnership of catechesis and religious education, of holiness and wholeness, could bring a life-giving depth and breadth to conversion in all its forms and to the meanings of maturity in faith and religious maturity. This book, then, seeks to postulate: 1) the catechetical meaning of conversion in the *National Directory for Catechesis* ought to be affirmed and nurtured, and, 2) the meaning of conversion disclosed in the literature of religious education adds depth and breath to it.

THE PROFESSIONS WITHIN THE CONTEXT OF CATECHESIS AND CONTEMPORARY RELIGIOUS EDUCATION

Within the context of both catechesis and contemporary religious education, attention needs to be drawn to the person(s) who is responsible for the educational programs and processes that are recognized in each field. The importance of the professional role of this person is acknowledged in both catechetical and religious education circles. Also acknowledged is an existing conflictual tension that infiltrates the professional identity of the fields and those who labor in them. For example, in referring to the role of the parish catechetical leader, the *National Directory for Catechesis* states: "Depending on the scope of responsibilities, the position is usually titled 'parish director of catechesis or religious education,' 'parish coordinator of catechesis or religious education,' or 'minister of catechesis or religious education.'"[34] In the landscape of Roman Catholic Church education, this person is commonly named the Director or Coordinator of Religious Education. However, in general, the *NDC* refers to the identity of this person as the Parish Catechetical Leader. This somewhat confused situation calls for an examination of the professional identity of those working in the context of church education.

Two professions, the profession of the Parish Catechetical Leader (PCL) in the catechetical field and the Director of Religious Education (DRE) in the field of contemporary religious education, can be seen working side by side in church education. Although religious education can function both inside and outside an ecclesial context (see Chapter 4), the focus of this examination will be on the professions of the DRE and PCL in the overall context of church education. We begin with the meaning of the term *professional*.

The Meaning of Professional

The term *professional* has always meant a person with special knowledge, who was especially dedicated. However, the meaning of the term has developed a historical pattern of its own. *Professional* originated in the medieval monastery where Christians made a profession of vows. A confession of faith was declared and they were professed as a grace or blessing. Living in a community, such persons were received by the whole church in a public ceremony. As professed persons and members of a religious order, they had privileges and duties that went beyond ordinary labors. Throughout medieval and pre-modern times, the professional, vowed in poverty, obedience, and chastity, was to 1) be ready to live in poverty; 2) be obedient to the life and goodwill of the community; and 3) be available for what has to be done, when it has to be done. Although this code was the embodiment of the professed of a religious order, the same essential code applied to the physician, lawyer, soldier, or statesman. Their kind of work was not considered a job, occupation, employment, or making a living, but was realized as doing what was right and good for that exact reason. [35]

The development of modernity caused a shift in the meaning of *professional*. Influenced by individualism, rational science, technology, and international trade, professionals now existed in increasingly narrow specializations while achieving money and status. Three points describe the new situation: 1) a "professional community" supplied individuals to local communities on a temporary basis; 2) the professional expected to get higher pay; and 3) professional knowledge and license gave them a protected status: the community was not to intrude.[36]

In the contemporary modern world, a near reversal has occurred from the original meaning of *professional*. While *professional* continues to claim the standards of special knowledge and dedication, the economic possibilities of having knowledge that others are in need of has been emphasized. Thus, being a professional has come to be something that is highly desirable. This represents a shift from its original meaning. Gabriel Moran explains the causes for the shift:

> Professionalism became entangled with the sexual, racial, and age bias present in the society. Having a professional career meant going up the narrow ladder of success. To be a professional now came to mean: 1) the possibility of earning big money, 2) independence from any and every community, and 3) control of time, place, and conditions for the exercise of one's highly specialized knowledge.[37]

Moran notes that in today's world society can no longer afford this shift in modern ideals to the present post-modern era. The former ideals could be sustained because they were realized by a smaller number of people who retained a residue of earlier attitudes. Society cannot bear the strain that is evoked from an attitude of interest in big money and maximum independence. But, for Moran, it is hopeless to offer a variation on poverty, obedience, and chastity in our present time. What Moran does offer is the possibility to work out a new synthesis that recovers some of the pre-modern attitude while retaining the real advances of the last century. He suggests a professional ideal in which: 1) the individual is able to support a family but has chosen work worth doing over the biggest paycheck possible; 2) the individual is capable of acting like an entrepreneur but chooses to work in a community or team of peers; and 3) the individual's technical skills are highly trained but are set within an attitude of reverence for living things and a recognition of human finitude.[38] Does this postmodern professional ideal have a place in the ecclesiastical setting? What influence would this ideal have in catechetical and religious educational settings? What implications does it hold for those persons who are responsible for the educational policies and processes that occur in these settings? In order to flesh out these queries, we turn now to the professions working in church education.

The Two Professions of Church Education

Two main forms of profession currently work in church education, namely, the profession of Religious Education and the profession of church ministry. These distinct but overlapping forms are not parallel professions but reflections of the different stages of historical development. The religious educator is a creation of the modern profession model. The church minister in education has characteristics of a pre-modern form of profession. Gabriel Moran claims that both professions can and should contribute to a post-modern form of church professionalism. We turn now to a description of both forms.

1) Religious Education—the hope of the Religious Education Association and movement in the early 1900s was to form an academic field and a profession. While this hope remains largely unfulfilled, the effort to realize a profession of religious education continues. In this endeavor, religious education professionals look to other branches of education for guidance and support. Their professional affiliation is with the world of education. The university, that certifies knowledge of both education and religion, supplies the credentials. The religious educator in a parish should expect a salary that is comparable to that of teachers and school-system administrators. A detailed contract would state the salary and terms of work. The developmental needs of the religious educator would include 1) a relationship with professional supporters in other parishes, religion teachers in Catholic and public schools, people in other Christian and non-Christian congregations, university and seminary faculties; 2) the recognition that a religious educator is not a church office but a profession that is free of the limitations of ecclesial structures; and 3) the realization that the religious educator's mission is to bring an educational critique to the existing church, including the very existence of parishes. Thus, the religious educator is marked by the modern concept of *professional* in its concern for specialized training, wider vision, and adequate pay. Religious educators, no matter where they are employed, should devote some of their time to people who have little money. Without accepting a low paying salary, they should publicly advertise that they are available for some of their working hours to those who can pay only a nominal fee.[39] This keeps them in touch with the original ideals of the professions. Professional religious educators, then, offer educational services to the churches. They work within the context of the parish/congregation but maintain their professional autonomy and distance. They are not ministers of the church.

2) Church Ministry in Education—this phrase describes the profession of many people in Protestant churches and Roman Catholic parishes. The profession of ministry provides their source of support as well as models of action. The church body supplies the credentials, and the individual's personal religious life may be considered more important than acquired academic degrees. A formal or informal sign of the community's consent takes the place of a legal contract. The church minister's loyalty is to the community and to its wide variety of demands. In return, the community should support the professional in various ways. While money is one legitimate sign of support, the rewards for this profession are not mainly financial. Gabriel Moran notes:

> The greater reward here is the recognition that one is using God-given talents to help others in educational ways. The main educational effort is to provide people with experiences of belonging to a Christian community. The aim is to

develop a community of communities, each with a competence that could be called professional.[40]

Hence, the profession of the church minister is marked by the pre-modern era in its commitment to the local community, sacrifice of financial rewards, and possible flexibility in defining membership.

In Roman Catholic circles, the responsibilities of the PCL are varied. The *National Directory for Catechesis* calls upon the help of Catholic colleges, universities, and organizations to provide potential parish catechetical leaders with opportunities to develop the competence and skills necessary for effective leadership and thorough knowledge of faith. The PCL, according to the *NDC,* also is required to be: 1) a fully initiated, practicing Catholic who fully adheres to the church's teaching in faith and morals; 2) a model of Christian virtue and a courageous witness to the Catholic faith; 3) prepared for service as a PCL in advanced studies in theology, Scripture, liturgy, catechesis and catechetical methodology, educational psychology and theory, and administration, as well as practical experience with adults, youth, and children; 4) comprehensively knowledgeable in the *General Directory of Catechesis* (1997) and the *Catechism of the Catholic Church;* and 5) a full member of the pastoral staff. In addition, the PCL should receive equitable compensation and opportunities for systematic training and study. She/he should continue with personal, spiritual, and professional development and should participate in diocesan programs of in-service training and formation, catechetical institutes, conventions, retreats, and accredited programs.[41]

This offering by the *NDC* may appear to include both the pre-modern and modern characteristics of a profession. However, is this contemporary meaning of the professional parish catechetical leader broad enough to be adequately posed in the climate of the post-modern professional? Is the *NDC* aware of the specific conflicts and tensions that affect the contemporary PCL? Is it necessary for parishes to recognize the distinction of both the DRE and the Church Minister in Education?

The strength of church ministry in education is that it exists and is flourishing in church circles.[42] Its weakness is that this system can be exploitive of good people and can be sexually biased. On the other hand, individual freedom of action and adequate recompense is the strength of religious education. Its weakness is that it barely yet exists. Efforts to develop a profession of religious education has had a checkered history. No solidified and lucid sense of professional identity has yet emerged. The rise and fall of the role of the Director of Religious Education (DRE) has been a victim of this checkered history.

The Rise and Fall of the DRE

As stated above, the hope of the Religious Education Association and the religious education movement in the early 1900's was to form an academic field and a profession. Filled with promise, the religious education movement was to evaluate, direct and coordinate a new "profession of religious education." However, at the same time in Protestant churches, there existed the growing sense of inadequacy and the need to meet the challenges of modernity. Thus, to meet these challenges, the new Director of Religious Education in the congregation began to appear in churches in 1909; the number of persons in this position continued to expand. Although serious attempts were made to clarify the work, role, and status of the parish director, these efforts were not completely successful. Kieran Scott describes the following situation that contributed to the demise of the DRE:

1) While the DRE was expected to bring the best of education to the life of the church, the position was always precarious and its educational work suspicious. Conflict existed between the minister and the director over questions of authority, areas of responsibility, and the nature of the activity.
2) Due to the subtle but significant change in the 1940s from liberal to neo-orthodox theology, the Director of Religious Education shifted titles to become Director of Christian Education. However, this change of title amounted to a shift in the identity of the profession. What transpired was that one profession (and field) went into decline while another reasserted itself. This signified the end of a hoped-for profession (DRE) and the beginning of a sub-profession (DCE). The emergence of *Christian education* implied that the professional role existed within the church's own profession, that is *ministry*.[43] In effect, the autonomous professional role of the DRE declined and became a form of church ministry.

The emergence of the professional DRE in the Roman Catholic Church occurred after the Second Vatican Council (1962-1965). Maria Harris notes that in the early 1970s, as well as today, the work of the DRE has been spoken of in terms of ministry as well as in terms of education. Use of these terms synonymously and interchangeably has caused an uncritical blurring of the two professions.[44] Such action can limit the attempts to organize and to move toward a distinct religious education profession. Kieran Scott warns that the present Catholic movement seems likely to follow the Protestant path. He states:

Many churches do not know what to expect from the DRE, and many DREs do not know what to expect from themselves. There is an acute lack of clear identity, confusion of roles and a blurred comprehension of the nature of their work. Ministry seems to be the first option of the majority. Few identify themselves, self-consciously, with the profession of religious education.[45]

The professional role of the DRE in both Protestant and Catholic churches has had an erratic journey. It is apparent that there is a need for a continuing conversation concerning the professional in contemporary church education. Could the implications of such conversation be beneficial? Can there be a partnering of the distinct roles of parish director of religious educator and church minister of education? Can the professional DRE in the Catholic parish learn from the downfall of the Protestant DRE? Can we learn from this history? Can we move toward a post-modern form of professional religious educator?

Implications of the Conversation

Maria Harris recognizes the distinction between church education and church ministry. She embraces the gifts of both. She is aware of the necessary tension between the two. Because of the latter, there is great temptation to collapse the two into one in the direction of ministry. Crediting communal and religious motives for a move from education to pastoral ministry, Harris, nevertheless, notes that there is a dark shadow side to this movement that may be the result of exhaustion, co-optation, or the desire to avoid conflict. Despite this, she hopes for a continuance of the ministry-education tension. Harris calls for both professions to be kept alive either within the person of the PCL/DRE and/or within the community where she or he works. She postulates:

> To me it is essential to champion the responsibilities, tribulations, sweat, and search for understanding that are proper to all critical education, at the same time that ministry by all members of the church is encouraged . . . DREs encourage ongoing education for all church members, taking seriously their own role as educators, they challenge those they educate to understand their baptismal vocations to ministry in the world. For the sake of the church, struggling to be its own best self, both professions are needed.[46]

Parishes can employ a church minister to direct or coordinate the educational resources of the community. Parishes also benefit from the challenge of the religious educator who respects current church structure, but does not assume it is forever cemented. With the contributions of both professions, professing Christians can give witness to the world of a renewed church. "This post-modern form of professionalism," Gabriel Moran states, "would draw upon the church's past, accept the history of modern times, and create for the future era communities of teaching and service."[47] Are both professions willing to partner to meet the educational challenges of the church in a post-modern world? Hopefully the recognition of the benefits that such a partnership would and could evoke will be finally realized.

THE INDISPENSABLE ROLE OF
TEACHING WITHIN THE FRAMEWORK OF
CATECHETICAL/EDUCATIONAL METHODOLOGIES

The *National Directory for Catechesis* offers *divine methodology* and *human methodology* as the two fundamental methods of communicating faith in catechesis and recognizes that *liturgical catechesis* provides a specific form of methodology.[48] *Liturgical catechesis* initiates believers into the Christian life and prepares the faithful for active participation in the church's liturgical celebrations. *Divine methodology* is the way the divine plan of God is revealed through the common work and action of the Triune God. Through the employment of *divine methodology*, catechesis is to deepen the believer's understanding of the mystery of Jesus Christ resulting in the believer's conversion to Jesus Christ and life of discipleship in Jesus Christ. The *NDC* also acknowledges the need for diverse human methodologies that organize the human element in the communion of faith. The directory offers elements to catechetical methodology that emphasize multiple forms of *learning*.[49] These forms are:

a) Learning through human experience—recognizes that human experiences, through the grace of the Holy Spirit, provide the sensible signs that lead a person to a better understanding of the truths of the faith.
b) Learning by discipleship - is centered on the person of Jesus Christ and the kingdom he proclaims. The hope is for the learner to become a disciple of Jesus by following his example.
c) Learning within the Christian community—emphasizes the role of family, parents, catechists, and particularly the parish in providing a locus where one's faith is nurtured and nourished.
d) Learning within the Christian family—avows the role of parents as primary educators in the faith and affirms the domestic church as a setting where the word of God is received and from which it is extended.
e) Learning through the witness of the catechist—places the catechist subsequently to the home and family as a pivotal witness to the gospel and realizes the catechist as a disciple of Christ within the catechetical process.

f) Learning by heart—acknowledges the need to memorize, absorb, and gradually understand, in depth, the faith traditions so they may become a source of Christian life on both the personal and communal levels.

g) Making a commitment to live the Christian life—advocates that active participation in Christian formation fosters learning by doing.

h) Learning by apprenticeship—underlines the importance of apprenticeship in its role of fostering an authentic following of Christ.[50]

These methodologies and forms of learning, presented in the *National Directory for Catechesis,* offer specific ways to communicate the traditions of the Catholic Church in relation to particular human experiences. While these methodologies contribute to the process of "handing on the faith," they are limited in scope. These limitations may inhibit a fuller, more enriched process for the learner as well as for the teacher. The educative process of teaching involves both the learner and the teacher. Why, then, are both the teacher and the learner not included in the section concerning catechetical methodologies in the *NDC*? Does such an approach short-circuit the educational process? By omitting academic teaching forms, does the *NDC* convey an imbalance in the process of teaching? Does catechesis equate the meaning of *teacher* with the meaning of *apprentice*? Can the field of contemporary religious education offer catechesis additional methods that might enhance the methodologies already offered?

Contemporary religious education is concerned also with a wider meaning of *teaching*. This concern includes the role of the teacher, but it underscores the relationship, the connectedness, and the process between teaching and learning. Such a process would include forms of teaching that are verbal and non-verbal. However, religious education also is concerned with the use of academic languages in teaching.[51] The meaning of teaching for religious education, especially as explored by Gabriel Moran, opens up a plurality of methods and processes that go beyond the catechetical methods offered in the *National Directory for Catechesis.* Therefore, it is essential that the role of *teaching/learning,* within the framework of catechetical/educational methodologies, be explored more deeply.

Teaching Within the Aims of Religious Education

"Teaching," Gabriel Moran states, " is one of the most important and regular acts that we perform in life."[52] Religious education can contribute a wider and deeper meaning of teaching by offering languages of teaching that are usually not seen in the modern philosophy of education. Religious education has two distinct and equally important aims: 1) to teach people to practice a religious way of life; and 2) to teach people to understand religion.[53]

The first aim of religious education is teaching people to practice a religious way of life. Contributions to this aim are the languages of storytelling and preaching. Important to every religion, these languages provide stories and origins of the past that support current practices. Equally important are the included languages of praise, thanks, confession, and mourning that provide emotional expression through celebratory rituals. Teaching emerges from the rituals themselves if the rituals are handed down. In showing a person how to practice a religious way, the teacher shows the way. The teacher here at times may be the whole community. Families are the first teachers to show the way. In the religious community, liturgy or worship is the chief teacher and the individual is taught by participating. This is catechesis. It remains oriented to the liturgy that teaches people the way to practice a religious life. The liturgy is where the lives of the participants are to be directed and inspired; if it is formative, its effect will trickle into social and political transformation within and beyond the parish.[54]

The second aim of religious education is: to teach people to understand religion. The starting point of this aim is the understanding of one's own religion. However, to understand is to compare, and to understand one's own religion is to compare one's religious perspective to that of another religion(s) or to no religion at all. The main language of this teaching form is academic speech. The classroom of the school is usually where this process takes place. We will turn now to explore in depth this distinctive teaching form.

Understanding through School Teaching and Academic Speech

The structure and the design of the classroom of the modern school sustain particular conditions that may be difficult to establish outside a school. It is set up to invoke a particular pattern of language, namely, academic discourse. Such language is needed for critical understanding.

Academic discourse is engaged by the schoolteacher to turn speech back on itself and to investigate its assumptions, biases, and meanings. Academic speech is not partisan and preachy. It allows for the examination of assumptions, contexts, and blind spots. It encourages one to temporarily put on hold one's own involvement and convictions.

At the same time, the schoolteacher advocates how to speak so that greater understanding is possible. She/he, however, does not tell people what to think but invites the learner to examine her/his way of speaking and understanding. The classroom, therefore, is a place for a particular kind of discourse that invokes 1) discussion that often takes the form of debate; 2) a sense of back and forth, of dialogue, with a reflective use of language; 3) particular attention directed to the meaning of the words in the dialogue; 4) an oral exchange that can only be fruitful if the participants are willing to listen to the words of the other, and the voice and otherness of an assigned text. A preachy and dogmatic attitude defeats the purpose of the classroom. On the other hand, good texts, teachers or students leave open the possibility of imagining different viewpoints and alternative worlds. Thus, classrooms are arenas of criticism. They cultivate an attitude of questioning everything. Kieran Scott explains:

> Academic speech, then, is concerned with meaning, with intellectual understanding. It questions the adequacy of every form of expression. Its form is interrogative. This critique, if it has communal support (within and outside the school), does not end in negativity. Rather, it can facilitate the emergence and flowering of new meaning and richer understanding. This is the purpose of classroom teaching. Consequently, when debate and criticism are absent, the classroom is simply not functioning as a genuine classroom.[55]

Thus, the classroom that supports academic inquiry is necessary for the richer understanding of one's religion and the religion of others. Religion, then, needs to be a field of academic inquiry.

Religion: A Field of Academic Inquiry

The term *religion*, however, has two distinct and very different meanings: 1) it is a word for a set of beliefs, rituals, and moral practices that particular communities engage in. It is a way a religious community shows a way of life, what one lives and practices; and 2) it is a word to designate a field of academic inquiry. We now focus on the second meaning.

Scholars who sought to study and compare religious communities invented the idea and concept of religion as a field of inquiry.[56] Like history, mathematics, social studies, and the health sciences, religion is an academic construct. While the aim and focus was to understand religion, a recent concept implies understanding one's religious position in relation to other possibilities. This concept claims religion can be a subject like any other in the school curriculum. "As an idea (of comparison) and as a method (of inquiry)," Kieran Scott notes, "it represents a commitment to use the mind in search for truth. The construct invites us to activate the muscles of the mind to explore, compare, question and critique."[57]

The appropriate place for this form of inquiry, according to Scott, is the modern classroom in the school.[58] Distinct from preaching a religious message, one teaches religion as part of an academic curriculum. While the schoolteacher is called to teach by example, she/he steps away from the personal practice of a particular way of religious life in order to examine the beliefs, sacred writings, and practice of other religious ways of life. The task of the schoolteacher is not to proselytize but to cultivate understanding. The task is not to tell people what the truth is or what to believe. The task for the schoolteacher is not to enrich the personal faith of the student but "to explore the meaning of what is written from the past and to help students articulate their own convictions."[59]

Unlike state schools in other countries that teach religion as an academic subject, most of the state schools of the United States do not. Reasons vary for this situation in the United States.[60] A presumption in the U.S. is that one can only teach religion in church (synagogue, mosque). Therefore, offering a religious education in the state or public school would be problematic. However, in spite of its absence, Gabriel Moran advocates that teaching religion has a place in the classrooms of the public schools in the United States.[61]

Church-related schools could offer rigorous, intellectually demanding accounts of religion. However, teachers in these schools, such as Roman Catholic schools, are asked to teach the teachings of the church accompanied by an affirmation of personal faith. Church-related schoolteachers are to "express an integrated approach to learning and living in their private and professional lives."[62] The *NDC* sanctions the catechetical formation of Catholic schoolteachers.[63] In other words, Catholic schoolteachers, like catechists in parish catechetical programs, are to share the same faith beliefs with their students; they are obligated to transmit these beliefs on their students. While this can be a positive and necessary event in certain contexts, do such assumptions inhibit the student's development toward the understanding of other religions? With such tenets in place, are church-related schools prevented from providing an academic environment where every statement is open to challenge, criticism, and reformulation? Does the concern for only one faith/belief invite "orthodoxy" or "heretical" concerns by church officials? For some educators, these questions are irrelevant in the academic classroom. The teacher of religion teaches the subject matter, teaches the student to think, and aids in the understanding of texts. It is the student's decision whether to affirm or dissent from this understanding. "The personal faith of the student or teacher," Scott notes, "is not an assumed part of the academic process nor its intended goal."[64] With this step, academic teaching goes beyond catechesis.

From this conversation, it is apparent that conflict could exist in the role of teaching within both the framework of catechetical methodologies and educational methodologies. While these roles bring distinct purposes to the conversation table, would their convergence offer a more creative, enriched practice and understanding to the process of teaching/learning? What are the implications of this conversation?

Implications of the Conversation

Contemporary religious education affirms catechesis and the contribution
it makes to a way of being religious in the world. However, due to the current milieu of catechesis, the two aims of religious education never meet.
Catechesis overlooks the second aim of religious education, namely, to teach
people to understand religion. It does not attend to religion as a field of academic inquiry. Likewise, academic instruction tends to be blind to the role
of catechizing.

Since academic instruction might not include the role of catechizing, could
or should an attempt be made to partner catechesis and religious education
within the context of teaching? Or should they be recognized and accepted
as being distinct and separate? Does contemporary catechesis do a disservice
to today's Catholic by not inviting one to understand one's own Catholic
traditions, symbols, rituals, and doctrines in an environment that utilizes
academic language and discourse? Do catechesis (and the Church) encourage
the Catholic living in a post-modern world, to seek understanding of other
religions through academic means? Apparently, the need to go beyond the
scope of catechesis and evangelization is crucial. Kieran Scott asserts that
the academic teaching of religion invokes universal, urgent, and practical
concerns for contemporary society. Scott states:

> The events of 11 September 2001 and its aftermath reveal that the main conflict
> in the world today is religious. Religion is not an innocent or a neutral force on
> the stage of history. The key question confronting us is: Will it be a life-giving
> force or will it turn deadly? A good starting point would be to seek to understand
> it. This is the unique contribution the teacher of religion can make to the current
> and next generation.[65]

In light of the contemporary climate of the world, the two aims of religious education cannot be ignored or separated. The practice of one's own
religion and the understanding of religion need to meet in the person of the
learner. Without this union, both the individual and society as a whole are
threatened. Therefore, the question arises: Is the field of catechesis, and, in
turn, is the Catholic Church willing to promote such a union? Do the ecumenical and inter-religious views of the church need to include going beyond
the development of an "appreciation of the insights of the adherents of other
religions and their contributions to humanity?"[66] How can catechesis seek to
"present the teachings of other churches, ecclesial communities, and religions
correctly and honestly"[67] if it does not provide an environment of academic
inquiry? The methodologies offered by catechesis contribute to a way of being religious in the world. However, teaching for the purpose of understand-

ing religion (one's own and others) is needed for the benefit of both teacher and learner on the journey toward religious understanding and practice. It is needed for the sake of the church and for the sake of the world.

RELIGIOUS PLURALISM IN THE THEOLOGICAL/RELIGIOUS FOUNDATIONS OF CATECHESIS AND RELIGIOUS EDUCATION

The theological foundations of catechesis and the religious foundations of religious education were explored in section 5 of Chapters 3 and 4. The matter of religious pluralism was not included in the exploration. However, this matter cannot be ignored or omitted in the discussion of the theological foundations of catechesis and the religious foundations of religious education or in the conversation between both fields.

Religious pluralism is the reality of a continued trend of the intermingling of cultures and religions that challenges the traditions of societies and religious institutions in our contemporary world. Wilbert R. Shenk gives an example of this situation. He notes: "Western societies that traditionally thought of themselves as Christian, with possibly a Jewish minority, today have become pluralistic. This is affecting how we carry on public discourse, interpret laws, teach religious and moral issues in public schools, and so forth."[68] Clearly, the developments of globalization and international terrorism raise searching interfaith questions in a secular world. These developments cry out for inter-religious dialogue if the planet is to survive.[69] Thus, religious pluralism and its effect(s) on world religions are raising theoretical and practical questions. The significance of this situation affirms that religious pluralism cannot be ignored in the conversation between religions and in the conversation between catechesis and religious education.

Religious communities need to question what impact these effects are having on their own general understanding of religious pluralism, on the position of their own religious traditions and foundations, and the stances of other religious traditions in light of this reality. Equally important is the speech used by various religious communities in communicating their theological and religious foundations and traditions. This scenario calls for the utilization of educational processes to help address this situation. Due to the significance of this current situation, the remainder of this book is concerned with the effects of religious pluralism on the theological and religious foundations within catechesis and religious education. We begin, however, with a sketch of the various theological positions that have emerged in the relationship of Christianity to other religious traditions.

Theological Positions toward World Religions

In light of the present circumstances, it has become necessary to work toward
an understanding among and between the various religions of the world. This
journey toward understanding, nevertheless, presents challenges for the multiple religious traditions that exist today. There is some consensus, however,
that there are major issues at stake here. There are also various options available for Christians.[70] These options tend to fall into three categories: exclusivism, inclusivism, and pluralism.

The major issues that are primarily traditional to Christians are: 1) Jesus
as the Christ is unique and that salvation comes only in his name; and 2) the
place and purpose of the church in the salvific process is called into question
if other religions can be recognized as vehicles of salvation for their members. Christian tradition had approached the latter with an ancient dictum:
there is no salvation outside the church. This view, that has come to be known
as *exclusivism,* sees little or no salvific value in other religions and affirms
church membership for salvific reasons. Another traditional Christian view of
salvation that has developed, namely, *inclusivism,* realizes the salvific power
of other religions. However, salvation is in and through the redemptive work
of Christ. In other words, this view claims that salvation is possible in other
religion traditions, but the ultimate means to the fullness of salvation is only
in and through Jesus Christ.[71]

Currently, some Christian theologians are attempting to develop another
position they name *pluralism.* This is a move away from the insistence that
Christ and Christianity are superior and absolute toward the recognition of the
independent validity of other ways. In other words, the salvation of people
can take place in other religious traditions without any relation to Jesus
Christ. T. Howland Sanks explains:

> This new view emphasizes God's universal salvific will and that grace is opera-
> tive in many ways. The Christian church is not the exclusive channel of grace
> or salvation. It is one of many paths. In this view, "Christianity is seen in a plu-
> ralistic context as *one* of the great world faiths, *one* of the streams of religious
> life through which human beings can be savingly related to that ultimate Reality
> Christians know as the heavenly Father." Each religious tradition is unique, but
> not absolute or superior to the others.[72]

The *pluralistic* position has invoked much discussion and controversy
among the Christian theological community. This perspective, in addition
to the *exclusivist* and *inclusivist* views, are the three major ways Christian
theologians are beginning to deal with the matter of religious pluralism.
The discussion is only at its beginning stage and will surely continue in
the future. As a central issue confronting Christianity today, religious

pluralism has certain implications for the Christian community's self-understanding.[73] These implications apply to the Roman Catholic tradition as well.

The Second Vatican Council (1962-1963) initiated the Catholic Church's openness to other faiths. This development has caused the Roman Catholic Church to deal with exclusivist, inclusivist, and pluralistic options in relation to other religions. It has experienced a shift from a pre-conciliar exclusivist view to a post-conciliar inclusivist position. In pluralistic terms, the question for today's church is: How does it adhere to its mission of proclaiming the Gospel to all nations while it engages in open and honest dialogue with other religious traditions at the same time? One way the church has dealt with this issue is to recognize and encourage interreligious dialogue. This posture, however, is viewed as an element of the church's evangelizing mission.[74] The Church also has warned against theological perspectives that are characterized by a religious relativism that leads to the belief that one religion is as good as another.[75] These perspectives continue to affect how the Catholic Church carries out its catechetical mission. In light of this affect, we turn now to the treatment of these perspectives in the *National Directory for Catechesis*.

The Stance on Religious Pluralism within the *National Directory for Catechesis*

In the chapter titled: "Catechesis in The Context of Ecumenical and Interreligious Dialogue," the *National Directory for Catechesis* describes within this context: 1) the view of a church founded by Jesus Christ; 2) the relationship of the Roman Catholic Church to other religions; and 3) the role of catechesis in the Catholic Church's ecumenical and interreligious efforts. This description also reflects some of the theological foundations of catechesis.

The Unity of the Church Founded by Jesus Christ

The *NDC* asserts that the church, founded by Jesus Christ, is one. The church is one because of the Trinity of Persons in one God. Through his sacrifice on the cross, Jesus Christ, the church's founder, has reconciled all persons to the Father. The Holy Spirit gathers the faithful into communion and joins them in the Body of Christ. The fundamental bond of the church's unity is charity that is expressed in the profession of one faith received from the apostles, the common celebration of the sacraments, and apostolic succession. The *NDC* continues: "This one Church is characterized by a great diversity that comes from the variety of God's gifts given to the Church and the diversity of those who receive them. This diversity, however, does not detract from the Church's essential unity. Rather, it is a dimension of her catholicity. While the directory maintains that Jesus has bestowed unity on the church, it also acknowledges that this unity has been wounded throughout history. To remedy this situation in our present time, the church calls for a continuance of prayer and work to maintain, reinforce, and "perfect the unity that Christ wills for her."[76] Are there any other directions the Catholic Church can take to remedy the situation? Other than its own unity, what additional concerns does or should the Catholic Church have in relation to ecumenism, interreligious dialogue, and religious pluralism?

Ecumenism

In an attempt to promote unity among all Christians, the *NDC* calls upon catechesis to foster ecumenical initiatives by maintaining an ecumenical dimension in its endeavors. It offers five catechesial principles for this purpose:

1) The Catholic Church brings its own gifts of self-understanding and the truth and gifts of grace given to the church by Christ. Catholics must have knowledge of the teachings and disciplines of the church and the Catholic principles of ecumenism if they are to engage in ecumenical activities.
2) Catechesis should engender and nourish an authentic desire for unity. It should employ serious efforts to remove any obstacles to unity. These efforts should include self-purification and renewal, and public and private dialogue and prayer.
3) Catechesis is to present the whole doctrine of the church with due regard to the hierarchy of truths. Such activity should honestly present, in a considerate manner, the differences but should prevent any obstacles to further dialogue.
4) Catechesis should present the teachings of the other churches, ecclesial communities, and religions in a correct and honest manner. It should recognize the divisions that exist among them, but catechesis should take steps to overcome them. By avoiding a misrepresentation of other Christians, Catholics can deepen their understanding of their own faith and develop genuine respect for the teaching of other faith communities. Catholics can then bear witness to the church's commitment of achieving unity among all Christians.
5) Catechesis prepares Catholics, in every stage of development, for living in contact with non-Catholics. This allows them to affirm their Catholic identity while respecting the faith of others. [77]

In order for these principles to be carried out, the *NDC* emphasizes the need for catechists to receive specialized training in ecumenism. They particularly are to be aware that the church, founded by Jesus Christ, "subsists in the Catholic Church."[78] Something of the Catholic Church can be found in other churches if they have preserved the revealed truth and gifts of grace given by "Christ to his Church." These churches are recognized by the *NDC* as existing in "some, though imperfect, communion with the Catholic Church."[79] Is this language conducive to ecumenical dialogue or does it show signs of a superior attitude on the part of the Catholic Church? Does it place the Catholic Church in danger of being isolated from other Christian traditions? What are the specific obstacles to unity, mentioned in the *NDC* that should be removed? What might other Christian religions think these obstacles are?

The *NDC* cautions that maintaining these basic catechesial principles can be quite challenging in the current situation of the day. This alleges that the church's missionary proclamation is endangered by relativistic theories that seek to justify religious pluralism. The revelation and mystery of Jesus Christ and the church, it warns, are in danger of losing their character of absolute truth and salvific universality.[80] It is in this context that it advocates that specialized training in ecumenism for catechists ought to include study of scripture and Catholic tradition; familiarity with the biblical foundations, historical knowledge and Catholic principles of ecumenism; training and experience in ecumenical collaboration and dialogue; familiarity with fundamental ecumenical issues; and participation in visits to other churches that would include informal exchanges, joint study days, and common prayer.[81]

Relations with Jews

The *NDC* also recommends that special care be given to catechesis in relation to the Jewish religion. This would entail a realization of the special organically integrated presence of the Jewish people within catechesis. Catechesis should uncover the ancient link between the church and the Jewish people, present precise, objective, and accurate teaching on the Jews and Judaism, and in particular, should serve to overcome every form of anti-Semitism. These objectives would help "Christians to appreciate and love the Jews, who were chosen by God to prepare for the coming of Christ."[82] Would Jews agree that this is their purpose and destiny? Is Judaism merely a preparation for the coming of Christ? Are volunteer catechists realistically capable of relaying accurate teaching about the Jews and Judaism? Would not an actively participating and knowledgeable Jew do this best? Could gaps in the knowledge of Judaism on the part of the catechist give way to "watering down" or "Christianizing" Jewish tradition and practice?

In order to attain a fundamental understanding of the history and traditions of Judaism, the *NDC* encourages catechists to 1) affirm both the Old and the New Testaments of the bible, recognizing the special meaning of the former; 2) show the independence and interconnectedness of both Testaments; 3) emphasize that Jesus' teachings reflect that he was a Jew; 4) respect the continuing existence of God's covenant with the Jewish people; and 5) show the Decalogue serves as a foundation of morality for both Christians and Jews. Could more not be done here? For example, could exposing the catechist and the catechized to actual Jewish practices, services, and museums foster a better understanding of the religious traditions of the Jewish people? Could Judaism be presented as an intact religious tradition in and of itself rather than a preparation for Christianity? What specific steps can be taken in order to expose the existence and the moral implications of anti-Semitism in both the past and immediate present?

Relations with Other Non-Christian Religions

The *National Directory for Catechesis* maintains that catechesis includes distinctive characteristics in relation to other non-Christian religions. It is the hope of the *NDC* that catechesis would "deepen and strengthen the identity of Catholics who encounter adherents to other religions and at the same time help them grow in respect for those believers and their religions."[83] In a religiously pluralistic society, it asserts: "It must always be taught clearly that Jesus Christ is the unique and universal Savior of the human family and that his Church is the universal sacrament of salvation."[84] While the church is to consider the goodness and truth found in the other faiths, these are to be seen as "a preparation for the Gospel."[85]

The *NDC* emphasizes the need for Catholics to become especially familiar with the history and elements of Islam, to work towards dialogue, mutual understanding, and cooperation with Islamic believers for the sake of social justice and moral welfare and peace and freedom. In order to promote respectful relationships with all non-Christian religions, fervent Catholic communities and well-formed catechists are encouraged to 1) offer an accurate account of the essential elements of non-Christian religious beliefs as perceived by the believers of these traditions and in light of their own religious experience; 2) develop an appreciation of the insights of and contributions to humanity by non-Christian believers; 3) promote joint projects in the cause of justice and peace; 4) foster a missionary spirit among those being catechized; and 5) motivate those being catechized to bear lively witness to the faith and to participate actively in the church's efforts to evangelize the world.[86]

The *NDC* acknowledges persons who join non-Christian religious or spiritual movements or cults are a particular important group for the church to evangelize. They are in need of a bold proclamation of the gospel for it contains answers to human questions.[87] In the conclusion of this chapter, it is claimed, "In this catechesis, the Church recognizes and celebrates the diversity within the community of faith, affirms the fundamental equality of every person . . . "[88] Does the Catholic Church actually do this? For example, the *NDC* declares: 1)"The message of salvation in Jesus Christ is intended for all people despite their social, cultural, racial, ethnic or economic differences"; 2) "The Church's catechesis presents the universal truth of the Gospel to every stratum of human society . . . with the resolute intention to transform all of society and renew the face of the earth"; and 3) "It (the church) adapts the Good News to the circumstances of all those who seek Christ in every part of the world while maintaining the unity of faith among all."[89] While the former statement reveals the church's desire to recognize those of other religious traditions, do the latter statements reveal that the mission of the church is to "Catholicize" those who do not yet participate in the Catholic faith tradition? Do the Roman Catholic Church's inclusivist, Christocentric perspectives hinder or promote understanding of other religious traditions? Does its stance contain a hidden religious imperialism? Is its position defensible in a context of religious pluralism?

The Role of Contemporary Religious Education within the Context of Religious Pluralism

In Chapter 4, section 5, the role of theology in the field of religious education and the relationship of one to the other were presented. Due to the religious need of our times, it was suggested that a bridge is needed between religions and religious language and non-religious speech. An educational approach to religion and an interreligious setting, where religious questions and concerns can be worked out, are at core to this endeavor. In this diverse religious world, religious education can be instrumental in interreligious dialogue.

Gabriel Moran calls for a wider, deeper, and endless conversation in religious education. He offers four guidelines for such a conversation, international, intergenerational, interinstitutional and interreligious. It is the interreligious that is most pertinent to the concern of religious pluralism. Inherent to religious education itself, an interreligious approach means understanding one's own religious position in relation to other religious possibilities.

According to Moran, a world of religious pluralism is not just a world of multiplicity. Religious pluralism is unlike the scenario where one religion considers itself as superior, or where the multiplicity of religions means less religious life. Religious pluralism of today demands that each religion be affirmed as important but only in relation to the others. Without an education that is genuine within each group and between groups, this demand certainly will fail.[90] Significant then are the two aims of religious education: 1) a better practice of one's own religious life and 2) a deeper understanding of another's religion.

Moran advocates that education is with end and without end. The former applies to all religious groups as they convey their way of life. The latter entails every major religious group has to recognize that there is a truth beyond whatever it has formulated. Moran explains:

> In every pronouncement, in every ritual, in every gesture toward the outsider, the religious group has to acknowledge its own incompleteness. The universal is embodied—but not completely—in the particular. The seeds not only of tolerance but of religious pluralism lie within the religions themselves.[91]

Religious education, therefore, plays an important role in the process of interreligious dialogue. Religious education de-absolutizes answers, even the best of religious answers that can be learned in school as well as within the other educational forms (family, work, and leisure). This learning is important because the mind needs to be stretched to its limits in order for it to make sense in describing a transcending of limits. For Moran, religious education is not about the building of one's case to score against one's adversaries. Rather it is relativizing one's religious tradition. That is placing it in relation to the religious lives of the other. Religious education, then, of its very nature has to be interreligious. In this regard, it goes beyond catechesis and enters a different paradigm.[92]

Implications of the Conversation

Some of the theological and religious foundations of the world's religions, or even the distortion of these foundations, have caused much of the catastrophic distress that has become part of the world's present landscape. If religion is a part of these problems, then, according to Dermot A. Lane, it must be part of the solution.[93] "There can be no peace among the nations," Hans Küng declares, "without peace among the religions. There can be no peace among religions without dialogue between religions. There can be no dialogue between religions without research into theological foundations."[94] It appears that religious education is invaluable for the process of dialogue and serves as a primary influence in the cause for world peace. It provides the framework for teaching, learning, and dialogue.

The three views that have emerged in addressing religious pluralism, namely, *exclusivity, inclusivity* and *pluralist* may have been helpful in constructing a theology of religions and opening up some dialogue. However, according to Dermot Lane, they have hit an impasse. Lane notes: "Pluralism and inclusivism, theologians point out, are (when scrutinized) expressions of an exclusivist position and therefore do not really promote dialogue"[95] If religions are serious about dialoguing with one another, they somehow need to move beyond this impasse. This means that catechesis, as presented in the *National Directory for Catechesis* needs to partner with religious education if authentic interreligious dialogue is to take place.

It can be said that the Catholic Church's relationship to other religions, since the Second Vatican Council, has become more receptive and outgoing. However, as Dermot Lane suggests, the Church must now move from an understanding of itself, as confined within a closed system, to one of being a tradition that properly belongs to an open and developing narrative. The Catholic Church is challenged to reconstruct itself in terms of an open narrative. It must "reconfigure itself as a faith that is open to critical engagement with the world, culture and other religions." [96] If the Catholic Church desires a fruitful interreligious encounter that will give rise to understanding, it must realize the need to promote the cultivation of hermeneutical sensibilities and a willingness to move beyond its limited horizons. Lane advises:

> To be religious in the present and the future will require that we be interreligious. Interreligious dialogue is no longer an optional extra, but rather an imperative arising out of the very nature of Christian faith itself. Further, the way of interreligious dialogue implies a new way of being Christian in the world and a new way of doing Christian theology. From now on, there is, as it were, a new way of describing Christian faith and a new source for the performance of Christian theology, namely, the encounter with other religions.[97]

Catechesis, in a context of a multicultural, religiously pluralistic world, has much to give as well as to gain through the encounter and authentic dialogue with other religious traditions. While catechesis cultivates religious roots and forms people in a better practice of Catholic religious life, it needs religious education to bring it to a deeper understanding of the religious life of the other. If catechesis, and, in turn, the Catholic Church, desire to take part in the global religious conversation, and be a part of the solution to the intense problems facing the world today, it has no choice but to partner with contemporary religious education.

SUMMARY

In this last chapter, the *National Directory for Catechesis* and contemporary religious education have been placed in a dialectical conversation. The purpose of this conversational inter-play was to: 1) address the absence of religious education in the *National Directory for Catechesis;* 2) determine the possible contributions a partnership with religious education could offer the field of catechesis; and 3) recognize what catechesis can contribute to the field of religious education.

Five sub themes within the prevailing five themes (in Chapters 3 and 4) have been addressed to capture the essence of each theme. This has been accomplished through: 1) The broadening of the meanings of catechesis and religious education through the acknowledgement of their respective identities; 2) The exploration of conversion in catechesis and religious education as an essential component of maturity in faith/religious maturity; 3) Addressing the professions that are pertinent to the context of catechesis and religious education; 4) Recognizing the indispensable role of teaching within the framework of catechetical/educational methodologies; and 5) Attending to religious pluralism in the theological/religious foundations of catechesis and religious education. The cornerstone for the conversation was provided by both the thematic content and tripartite purpose of the *NDC*, namely 1) to provide fundamental theological and pastoral principles drawn from the Church's magisterium and to apply them to the pastoral activity of catechesis; 2) to offer guidelines for the application of those fundamental theological and pastoral principles in this country in order to promote a renewal of catechesis; and 3) to set forth the nature, purpose, object, tasks, basic content, and various methodologies of catechesis.[98] In addition, some practical and pastoral implications of the dialectical conversations were presented.

Hopefully such an endeavor would contribute, not so much to the collapse of tension between catechesis and religious education, but that the tension be a creative one. The positive results of these conversations reveal that a partnership of both fields would enrich the educational processes of catechesis and the life of the church. But no conversation can take place if one partner is absent. This has been the thesis of this book.

NOTES

1. For example, see the *National Directory for Catechesis,* no. 54, sect. 9a.

2. *National Directory for Catechesis,* no. 5.

3. Thomas Groome. *What Makes Us Catholic: Eight Gifts for Life* (San Francisco: HarperCollins, 2002), xix.

4. Gabriel Moran. *Religious Education As A Second Language* (Birmingham: Religious Education Press, 1989), 12.

5. Kieran Scott. "A Middle Way: The Road Less Traveled" *The Living Light* 37, no. 4 (2001): 43.

6. Scott. "A Middle Way: The Road Less Traveled," 43.

7. Kieran Scott. "Three Traditions of Religious Education" *Religious Education* 79, no. 3 (1984): 326.

8. *National Directory for Catechesis,* no.51.

9. Moran, *Religious Education as a Second Language,* 27.

10. Moran, *Religious Education as a Second Language,* 23.

11. Moran, *Religious Education as a Second Language,* 29.

12. Scott, "Three Traditions of Religious Education," 333.

13. Scott, "Three Traditions of Religious Education," 333.

14. Scott, "Three Traditions of Religious Education," 327.

15. Jack L. Seymour. "The Future of the Past: History and Policy-Making in Religious Education" *Religious Education,* 81, no. 1 (1986): 115.

16. *National Directory for Catechesis,* no. 48, sect. A.

17. Gabriel Moran, *Religious Education Development: Images for the Future.* (Minneapolis: Winston Press, 1983) 150-51.

18. *National Directory for Catechesis,* no. 17, sect. A.

19. *National Directory for Catechesis,* no. 29, sect. A.

20. *National Directory for Catechesis,* no. 17, sect. B.

21. *National Directory for Catechesis,* no. 36, sect. A.

22. *National Directory for Catechesis,* no. 35, sect. D.

23. Mary C. Boys, "Conversion as a Foundation of Religious Education" in *Religious Education,* 77 no. 2 (1982): 212.

24. Boys, "Conversion as a Foundation of Religious Education" 212-13.

25. Boys, "Conversion as a Foundation of Religious Education" 216-17.

26. Boys, "Conversion as a Foundation of Religious Education" 217-23.

27. Boys, "Conversion as a Foundation of Religious Education" 223-24.

28. Moran, *Religious Education Development: Images for the Future*, 95.

29. Moran, *Religious Education Development*, 95.

30. Moran, *Religious Education as a Second Language,* 145.

31. Moran, *Religious Education as a Second Language,* 146.

32. Austin Flannery, "Dogmatic Constitution on the Church." *Vatican Council II Vol. 1: The Conciliar and Post Conciliar Documents* (Northport: Costello Pub. Co.1996) no. 40.

33. Scott, "A Middle Way: The Road Not Traveled," 40-41.

34. *National Directory for Catechesis,* no. 54, sect. B-5.

35. Moran, *Religious Education as a Second Language,* 202-03.

36. Gabriel Moran, *Interplay: A Theory of Religion and Education* (Winona: St. Mary's Press, 1981), 93.

37. In *Religious Education as a Second Language,* Moran acknowledges Burton Bledstein's *The Culture of Professionalism* (New York: Norton, 1976), 203.

38. Moran, *Religious Education as a Second Language,* 204.

39. Moran, *Interplay,* 96-98.

40. Moran, *Interplay,* 99.

41. *National Directory for Catechesis,* no 54, sect. B-5.

42. See the United States Conference of Catholic Bishops, *Co-Workers in the Vineyard of the Lord* (December, 2005).

43. Kieran Scott. "Religious Education and Professional Religious Education: A Conflict of Interest?" in *Religious Education,* 77 no. 6 (1982): 602.

44. Maria Harris, "U.S. Directors of Religious Education in Roman Catholic Parishes" in *Changing Patterns of Religious Education,* ed. Marvin J. Taylor, 215 (1984).

45. Scott, "Religious Education and Professional Religious Education: A Conflict of Interest?" 603.

46. Harris, "U.S. Directors of Religious Education in Roman Catholic Parishes," 215-16.

47. Moran, *Interplay,* 100.

48. See Chapter 3, section 4 of the *National Directory for Catechesis.*

49. The role of catechesis within these forms is presented in Chapter 3 of this book, section 4.3.

50. *National Directory for Catechesis,* no. 29, sect. A-H.

51. See Chapter 4, section 4 of the *National Directory for Catechesis.*

52. Moran, *Reshaping Religious Education,* 32.

53. See Chapter 4, section 1.5 of the *National Directory for Catechesis.*

54. Moran, *Religious Education as a Second Language,* 146.

55. Kieran Scott, "The Schoolteacher's Dilemma: To Teach Religion or Not To Teach Religion?" in *Critical Issues in Religious Education* ed. Oliver Brennan, 71 (Dublin: Veritas, 2005).

56. Scott, "The Schoolteacher's Dilemma," 72.

57. Scott, "The Schoolteacher's Dilemma," 73.

58. Scott, "The Schoolteacher's Dilemma," 73.

59. Scott, "The Schoolteacher's Dilemma," 75.

60. See Moran in *Religious Education As A Second Language,* Chapter 5, 114-37.

61. Moran, *Religious Education As A Second Language,* 138.

62. *To Teach As Jesus Did* in *The Catechetical Documents: A Parish Resource* (Chicago: Liturgy Training Publications, 1996) no. 104.

63. *National Directory for Catechesis,* no. 48, sect. A.

64. Scott, "The Schoolteacher's Dilemma" 75.

65. Scott, "The Schoolteacher's Dilemma," 67-68.

66. *National Directory for Catechesis,* no. 51, sect. E.

67. *National Directory for Catechesis,* no. 51, sect. B.

68. Wilbert R. Shenk, cited in "The Challenge of Religious Pluralism" by Norma H. Thompson in *Religious Pluralism and Religious Education* ed. Norma H. Thompson, (Birmingham: Religious Education Press, 1988) 9.

69. Dermot A. Lane, "Christian Faith in the Context of a Multicultural World" *The Living Light,* 40 no. 4 (2004) 68-71.

70. T. Howland Sanks, *Salt, Leaven and Light: The Community Called Church* (New York: Crossroads, 1992) 233.

71. Sanks, *Salt, Leaven and Light*, 233-34.

72. Sanks, *Salt, Leaven and Light*, 234.

73. Sanks, *Salt, Leaven and Light*, 235.

74. Sanks, *Salt, Leaven and Light*, 236.

75. See Pope John Paul II, encyclical, *Redemptoris Missio*, (1991).

76. John Paul II, *Redemptoris Missio*.

77. *National Directory for Catechesis*, 51, sect. B.

78. The *National Directory for Catechesis*, (no. 51, sect C) is citing the *Catechism of the Catholic Church* no. 816 that, in turn, cites Lumen gentium, no. 8.

79. *National Directory for Catechesis*, no. 51, sect. C.

80. *National Directory for Catechesis*, no. 51, sect. C.

81. *National Directory for Catechesis*, no. 51, sect. C.

82. *National Directory for Catechesis*, no. 51, sect. D.

83. *National Directory for Catechesis*, no. 51, sect. E.

84. *National Directory for Catechesis*, no. 51, sect. E.

85. *National Directory for Catechesis*, no. 51, sect. E.

86. *National Directory for Catechesis*, no. 51, sect. E.

87. *National Directory for Catechesis*, no. 51, sect. E.

88. *National Directory for Catechesis*, no. 51, sect. E.

89. *National Directory for Catechesis*, no. 52.

90. Moran, *Religious Education as a Second Language*, 229.

91. Moran, *Religious Education as a Second Language*, 232.

92. Moran, *Religious Education Development*, p. 205.

93. Lane, "Christian Faith in the Context of a Multicultural World," 69.

94. Hans Küng cited in Dermot A. Lane, "Christian Faith in the Context of a Multicultural World," 69.

95. Lane, "Christian Faith in the Context of a Multicultural World," 71.

96. Lane, "Christian Faith in the Context of a Multicultural World," 77.

97. Lane, "Christian Faith in the Context of a Multicultural World," 80.

98. *National Directory for Catechesis*, no. 5.

Conclusion

This book has been an attempt to search for an element that intuitively appears to be absent and elusive in the field of catechesis, as represented in the *National Directory for Catechesis.*

The frequent interchanging of the terms *catechesis* and *religious education,* by ecclesial members, professionals, and leaders, appears to imply that both terms are synonymous in meaning, purpose, and implications. However, a task of this author was to determine whether catechesis and religious education are equally significant and distinct enterprises. Through some preliminary research, it was determined that these fields are distinct in their histories, purposes, methodologies, and theological foundations. In addition, after an in-depth study of the *National Directory for Catechesis,* it became apparent that not only was religious education distinct from catechesis, it did not exist in collaboration with the catechetical endeavors of the Roman Catholic Church. The metaphor of an "absent partner" was chosen to describe religious education within this context.

While the catechetical enterprise is to be affirmed for its contribution to the teaching ministry and mission of the Roman Catholic Church, the next task was to determine if the absent partner, religious education, could become a visible and viable partner with catechesis in the process of religiously educating contemporary and future Catholic disciples in the United States. Would such a partnership be beneficial to catechesis, to religious education or to both? It was the hope of this author to realize a positive answer to this question. Such a response could possibly encourage a more enriching catechetical and religiously educational experience for the person and the parish community. This, in turn, would offer the possibility of benefiting the universal church's mission and ministry as well.

This book brings copious information to process and digest and, yet, it has its limitations. I have not addressed particular issues that still call for further discussion and research. Some of these issues include: 1) the legal dimensions of including religious education in public schools; 2) some specific curricular issues; 3) theories/models of revelation; 4) the role of various pedagogical processes used by Jesus, the teacher; 5) a probing of additional educational methodologies that could enhance the teaching-learning process such as *service learning*; 6) further study in the role of social sciences that might include *emotional intelligence* in the educational process; and 7) specific information concerning ecumenical and interreligious dialogue within the context of religious pluralism.

This study concludes that catechesis and religious education remain distinct enterprises. A melding together of the two would risk a loss of the specific identity of each and their particular contributions toward educating for a religious way of life. What is needed is the continuance of a healthy tension that invites each to become more enriched, enhanced, renewed, and life-giving. This book is an invitation for catechesis and religious education to generate a continuous healthy dialogue, while maintaining their distinctiveness. The hope is this work is a contribution to that endeavor.

This book has presented the need for religious education and catechesis to meet in dialogue. The words of Hanan A. Alexander remind us of this notion. He writes:

> It is often this strange and often uncomfortable blend of devotion to God and tradition on the one hand and uncompromising willingness to follow questions wherever they may lead on the other that has been the hallmark of the religious education movement . . . religion and education in the deepest sense are not about exercising control over others in the name of God or history or liberation or anything else; they are about learning to exercise control over ourselves, by letting God or tradition or sanctity or some other form of high ethical ideals, however we have come to understand them, into our hearts.1

Together, catechesis with religious education, could contribute to this hope. For the sake of the church and of the world, may a serious dialogue begin. But dialogue requires the presence of two partners.

NOTE

1. Hanan A. Alexander, "Against the Grain: Religious Education at 100" in *Religious Education,* 100, no. 4 (2005): 356.

Bibliography

PRIMARY SOURCES

Level I

National Directory for Catechesis. United States Conference of Catholic Bishops. Washington, D.C.: 2005.

Level II

Universal Ecclesial Documents

Catechism of the Catholic Church. Second Edition. United States Catholic Conference—Libreria Editrice Vaticana, 1997.

Congregation for the Clergy. *General Directory for Catechesis.* Libreria Editrice Vaticana, 1997.

General Catechetical Directory (1971). *The Catechetical Documents: A Parish Resource.* Chicago: Liturgy Training Publications, 1996.

Pope John Paul II, "On Catechesis in Our Time" (1979). *The Catechetical Documents: A Parish Resource.* Chicago: LiturgyTraining Publications, 1996.

Pope Paul VI, "Evangelii Nuntiandi" (1975) *The Catechetical Documents: A Parish Resource.* Chicago: LiturgyTraining Publications, 1996.

National Ecclesial Documents

Basic Teachings for Catholic Religious Education (1973). *The Catechetical Documents: A Parish Resource. Chicago: Liturgy Training Publications, 1996.*

Our Hearts Were Burning Within Us: A Pastoral Plan for Adult Faith Formation in the United States. Washington: United States Catholic Conference, 1999.

Sharing the Light of Faith: National Catechetical Directory for Catholics of the United States. United States Catholic Conference, Department of Education, 1979.

To Teach As Jesus Did (1972). *The Catechetical Documents: A Parish Resource.* Chicago: Liturgy Training Publications, 1996.

SECONDARY SOURCES

The Aims of Religious Education. The Proceedings of the Third Annual Convention of the Religious Education Association, Boston. Chicago: Religious Education Association, 1905.

Alexander, Hanan A. "Against the Grain: Religious Education at 100." *Religious Education,* 100:4, Fall, 2005.

Barker, Kenneth R. *Religious Education, Catechesis, and Freedom.* Birmingham: Religious Education Pub., 1981.

Boys, Mary C. "Conversion as a Foundation of Religious Education." *Religious Education,* 77:2, March-April 1982.

—— *Educating in Faith: Maps and Visions.* Lima: Academic Renewal Press, 1989.

—— "Teaching: The Heart of Religious Education." *Religious Education Journal* 79:2, Spring, 1984.

—— "The Role of Theology in Religious Education." *Horizons,* 11:1, 1984.

Bryce Mary Charles. "The Baltimore Catechism—Origin and Reception." *Sourcebook for Modern Catechetics.* ed. by Michael Warren. Winona: Saint Mary's Press, 1983.

—— *Pride of Place: The Role of the Bishops in the Development of Catechesis in the United States.* Washington, D.C.: The Catholic University of America Press, 1984.

—— "*Sharing the Light of Faith*: Catechetical Threshold for the U.S. Church." *Sourcebook for Modern Catechetics.* ed. Michael Warren. Winona: St. Mary's Press, 1983.

Bushnell, Horace. *Christian Nurture.* New Haven: Yale University Press, 1967.

Coe, George Albert. *A Social Theory of Religious Education.* New York: Scribner, 1917.

—— *What is Christian Education?* New York: Scribner, 1929.

Collins, Joseph B. "The Beginnings of the CCD in Europe and Its Modern Revival." *Sourcebook for Modern Catechetics.* ed. by Michael Warren. Winona: Saint Mary's Press, 1983.

—— "Bishop O'Hara and a National CCD." *Sourcebook for Modern Catechetics.* ed. by Michael Warren. Winona: Saint Mary's Press, 1983.

—— "Religious Education and CCD in the United States: Early Years (1902–1935)." *Sourcebook for Modern Catechetics.* ed. by Michael Warren. Winona: Saint Mary's Press, 1983.

Cope, Henry F. "Ten Years Progress." *Religious Education,* 8:2 June, 1913.

Cunnane, Finola. "Issues of Identity in Religious Education." *Critical Issues in Religious Education.* ed. Oliver Brennan. Dublin: Veritas, 2005.

Dolan, Jay. *The American Catholic Experience: A History from Colonial Times to the Present.* Notre Dame: University of Notre Dame, 1992.

Dooley, Catherine. "Evangelization and Catechesis" in *The Echo Within: Emerging Issues in Religious Education.* Allen, TX: Thomas More, 1997.

Elbe, Kenneth. *The Craft of Teaching.* San Francisco: Jossey-Bass, 1976.

Elias, John L. *A History of Christian Education: Protestant, Catholic, and Orthodox Perspectives.* Malabar: Krieger Pub. Co., 2002.

—— "Catholics in the REA, 1903–1953." *Religious Education Journal 99:3,* Summer, 2004.

Flannery, Austin. *Vatican Council II Vol. 1: The Conciliar and Post Conciliar Documents.* Northport: Costello Pub. Co., 1996.

Fowler, James W. *Stages of Faith: The Psychology of Human Development and the Quest For Meaning.* San Francisco: Harper, 1981.

Go and Make Disciples: A National Plan and Strategy for Catholic Evangelization in the United States. Washington, D.C.: National Conference of Catholic Bishops, November 18, 1992.

Groome, Thomas. *Christian Religious Education: Sharing Our Story and Vision.* San Francisco: Jossey-Bass, 1980.

—— "Parish as Catechist" in *Church,* Fall, 1990.

—— *What Makes Us Catholic: Eight Gifts for Life.* San Francisco: HarperCollins, 2002.

Groome, Thomas and Horell, Harold Daly. *Horizons and Hopes: The Future of Religious Education.* Mahwah: Paulist Press, 2003.

Harris Maria. *Fashion Me a People: Curriculum in the Church.* Louisville: Westminster John Knox, 1989.

—— "U.S. Directors of Religious Education in Roman Catholic Parishes." *Changing Patterns of Religious Education.* ed. Marvin J. Taylor. Nashville: Abington, 1984.

Harris, Maria and Moran, Gabriel. *Reshaping Religious Education: Conversations on Contemporary Practice.* Louisville: Westminster John Knox Press, 1998, p. 18.

Heath, Mark. "To Teach As Jesus Did: A Critique" in *The Living Light, 10:2,* Summer, 1973.

Horan, Michael P. "Overview of the General Catechetical Directory: Historical Context and Literary Genre". *The Catechetical Documents: A Parish Resource.* Chicago: Liturgy Training Publications, 1996.

—— "Introduction to the *Catechism of the Catholic Church." The Catechetical Documents: A Parish Resource.* Chicago: Liturgy Training Publications, 1996.

In Support of Catechetical Ministry: A Statement of the U.S. Bishops. Washington, D.C.: United States Catholic Conference, Inc., 2000.

John Paul II. *Redemptoris missio.* Encyclical, December 12, 1990.

Jones, Howard Mumford. "Development in Humanistic Scholarship." *Both Human and Humane.* eds. C.E. Bolwe and R.F. Nichols. Philadelphia: University of Pennsylvania, 1960.

Kelcourse, Felicity B. "Theories in Human Development." *Human Development and Faith: LifesCycle Stages of Body, Mind, and Soul.* ed. Felicity B. Kelcourse. St. Louis: Chalice Press, 2004.

La Cugna, Catherine M. *God For Us: The Trinity and Christian Life.* San Francisco: Harper, 1991.

Lane, Dermot A. "Christian Faith in the Context of a Multicultural World." *The Living Light,* 40:4, Summer, 2004.

Lee, James Michael. "The Authentic Source of Religious Instruction." *Religious Education and Theology.* ed. Norma H. Thompson. Birmingham: Religious Education Press, 1982.

Marthaler, Berard L. "The Modern Catechetical Movement in Roman Catholicism" in *Sourcebook for Modern Catechetics.* ed. by Michael Warren. Winona: Saint Mary's Press, 1983.

—— "Socialization as a Model for Catechetics" in *Sourcebook for Modern Catechetics, Volume 2.* ed. by Michael Warren. Winona: Saint Mary's Press, 1997.

Miller, Randolph Crump. *The Clue to Christian Education.* New York: Scribner, 1950.

Mongoven, Anne Marie. "The Directory: A Word for the Present" in *The Living Light, 16:2,* Summer, 1979.

—— "The Directories as Symbols of Catechetical Renewal." *The Echo Within: Emerging Issues in Religious Education.* ed. Catherine Dooley. Allen, TX: Thomas Moore, 1997.

Moran, Gabriel. "Catechetics in Context . . . Later Reflections" in *Sourcebook for Modern Catechetics.* ed. by Michael Warren. Winona: Saint Mary's Press, 1983.

—— "From Obstacle to Modest Contributor: Theology in Religious Education." *Religious Education and Theology.* ed. Norma H. Thompson. Birmingham: Religious Education Press. 1982.

—— *Interplay: A Theory of Religion and Education.* Winona: St. Mary's Press, 1981.

—— "The Intersection of Religion and Education." *Religious Education 69:5,* September-October, 1974.

—— *Religious Education as a Second Language.* Birmingham: Religious Education Press, 1989.

—— "Religious Education After Vatican II." *Open Catholicism: The Tradition at Its Best.* eds. David Efroymson and John Raines. Collegeville: The Liturgical Press, 1997.

—— *Religious Education Development: Images for the Future.* Minneapolis: Winston Press, 1983.

—— *Showing How: The Act of Teaching.* Valley Forge: Trinity Press International, 1997.

—— "Two Languages of Religious Education." *The Living Light, 14:1,* Spring, 1977.

—— "Understanding Religion and Being Religious." *Pace* 21, 1992.

New American Catholic Bible, Personal Study Edition. New York: Oxford University Press, 1995.

The New Oxford American Dictionary. New York: Oxford University Press, 2001.

Quinn, John M. "National CCD Congresses Shaped Catechesis in the United States" in *The Living Light, 39:4,* Summer, 2003.

Regan, Jane. "Overview of *On Catechesis In Our Time.*" *The Catechetical Documents: A Parish Resource.* Chicago: Liturgy Training Publications, 1996.

—— "Overview of *Basic Teachings for Catholic Religious Education.*" *The Catechetical Documents: A Parish Resource.* Chicago Liturgy Training Publications, 1996.

Sanks, T. Howland. *Salt, Leaven and Light: The Community Called Church.* New York: Crossroads, 1992.

Sawicki, Marianne. "Historical Methods and Religious Education" in *Religious Education, 82:3,* Summer, 1987.

Scott, Kieran. "The Schooteacher's Dilemma: To Teach Religion or Not To Teach Religion?" ed. Oliver Brennan. *Critical Issues in Religious Education.* Dublin: Veritas, 2005.

——A Middle Way: The Road Not Traveled" in *The Living Light 37:4,* Summer, 2001.

—— "Religious Education and Professional Religious Education: A Conflict of Interest?" *Religious Education, 77:6,* November/December, 1982.

—— "Three Traditions of Religious Education" in *Religious Education. 79:3,* Summer, 1984.

Shenk, Wilbert R. in a review of S. Mark Heim, *Is Christ the Only Way? Christian Faith in a Pluralistic World.* Valley Forge: Judson Press, 1985 in *International Bulletin of Missionary Research* 11:2, April, 1987.

Smith, H. Shelton. *Faith and Nurture.* New York: Charles Scribner's Sons, 1950.

Thompson, Norma H. "The Role of Theology in Religious Education: An Introduction." *Religious Education and Theology.* ed. Norma H. Thompson. Birmingham: Religious Education Press, 1982.

—— "The Challenge of Religious Pluralism." *Religious Pluralism and Religious Education.* ed. Norma H. Thompson. Birmingham: Religious Education Press, 1988.

United States Conference of Catholic Bishops. Office of Media Relations. January 13, 2005, http://www.usccb.org.

"USCCB Hosts National Symposium on *National Directory for Catechesis.*" National Conference for Catechetical Leadership. No. 9, January 13, 2005m http://www.nccl.org.

Walsh, Richard W. in "Overview of *To Teach As Jesus Did.*" *The Catechetical Documents: A Parish Resource.* Chicago: Liturgy Training Publications, 1996.

Walters, Thomas P. "Overview of *Evangelization in the Modern World.*" *The Catechetical Documents: A Parish Resource.* Chicago: Liturgy Training Publications, 1996.

Warren, Michael. "A New Priority in Pastoral Ministry" in *The Living Light, 37:1,* Fall, 2000.

—— "Catechesis: An Enriching Category for Religious Education" in *Sourcebook for Modern Catechetics.* ed. by Michael Warren. Winona: Saint Mary's Press, 1983.

Westerhoff, John H. *Who Are We?: In Search of an Identity.* Birmingham: Religious Education Press, 1978.

Wuerl, Bishop Daniel. "A Look Inside the New U.S. Catechetical Directory" in *Origins 34:33,* February 3, 2005.

Wyckoff, D. Campbell. *The Task of Christian Education.* Philadelphia: The Westminster Press, 1955.

Zaums, John R. "Overview of *Sharing the Light of Faith: National Catechetical Directory for Catholics of the United States."* *The Catechetical Documents: A Parish Resource.* Chicago: Liturgy Training Publications, 1996.

Index

absolutism, 31
academic discourse, 135–36
adolescence. *See* life stages
adult faith formation, xii, 11–17, 56–57, 60–61. *See also* Rite of Christian Initiation for Adults
American Sunday School Union, 26
anthropology, Christian, 77–78
apprenticeship, 72, 134

Baltimore Catechism, 6
baptism, 25, 74
baptismal catechumenate, 74
Barker, Kenneth R., 30, 37, 40
Barth, Karl, 36
Basic Teachings for Catholic Religious Education (1973), xii, 12–14
Beatitudes, 58
Bible: adult education, 58; approaches to, 28–29, 34–38; centrality, 39–40, 50–53
Bible Theology Movement, 38
bishops, 64, 68
Bower, William Clayton, 34
Boys, Mary, 22, 25, 28, 31, 34–36; on conversion, 123–25; on James Smart, 40; theology, 108–9
Bruggemann, Walter, 120

Bryce, Mary Charles, 2, 4, 10–12; on Church documents, 13, 15
Bushnell, Horace, 25–26

Can Religious Education Be Christian? (1940), 37
Canisius, Peter, 4
Carroll, John (Bishop), 4–5
Catechesi Tradendae (1979), xiii, 47, 49
catechesis: adult, 56–57; aims, 142–43; and modern education, 18; context, 61–63; definition, ix, 1, 47; four tasks, 15; Gospel and world, 16; identity, 119, 121–22; initiatory, 59; language of, 17; leaders, 65, 126–27, 129–30; liturgical, 69; methodology, 47, 58–59, 69–71; ongoing, 59–60; phases, 52; pluralism, 147; vs. religious education, x, 18–19, 42–43; renewal, 7–11, 46–47; Second Vatican Council, xii; six resolutions, 11; stages, 60; tasks, 53. *See also* catechists; conversion; evangelization; history; leaders
"Catechesis in Our Time" (1977 synod), 12
Catechism of the Catholic Church (1992), xiii, 57–58, 75

Breinigsville, PA USA
29 April 2010
237033BV00003B/1/P